Animals and Man

The Romanes Lecture for 1984–5
Delivered in Oxford on 5 February 1985

MIRIAM ROTHSCHILD

CLARENDON PRESS · OXFORD
1986

Oxford University Press, Walton Street, Oxford OX2 6DP
Oxford New York Toronto
Delhi Bombay Calcutta Madras Karachi
Petaling Jaya Singapore Hong Kong Tokyo
Nairobi Dar es Salaam Cape Town
Melbourne Auckland
and associated companies in
Beirut Berlin Ibadan Nicosia

Oxford is a trade mark of Oxford University Press

Published in the United States
by Oxford University Press, New York

British Library Cataloguing in Publication Data
Rothschild, M.
Animals and man: the Romanes lecture for
1984–5 delivered in Oxford on 5 February
1985.
1. Animals, Treatment of
I. Title
179'.3 HV4708
ISBN 0-19-854210-0

Set by Grestun Graphics, Abingdon, Oxon.
Printed in Great Britain by
Biddles Ltd.,
Guildford and King's Lynn

To the Memory of Alix's Dog

ACKNOWLEDGEMENTS

A number of my friends and acquaintances have helped me write this book, but in particular I must thank Richard Harrison and Ruth Harrison for the infinite trouble they have taken over the chapter on Farming, and Vince Dethier and Robert Hinde for assistance with the chapter on the Laboratory. Alistair Worden and Harry Thompson gave me useful advice and excellent references for the Countryside Chapter. I am also most grateful to all those who read parts of the manuscript, corrected various errors, discussed and advised me on different points of view, and gave me factual information as well as various books and papers to read. For these multiple kindnesses I would like to thank William Allen, Miriam Balaban, Gunnar Bergström, B. Berkovits, Isaiah Berlin, John Butterfield, Marian Dawkins, Vince Dethier, Susan Duncan, Dayan Ehrentreu, Arthur Fried, Jo Gillies, Alister Hardy, William Henderson, Robert Hinde, Clive Hollands, Gill Kerby, John Krebs, Nancy Lane, Katya Lester, Leo Levi, Elisabeth Luard, Asher Meshorer, Alastair Mews, Cindy Milburn, Albert Neuberger, Julia Neuberger, Rozsika Parker, Philip Pick, Len Rutherford, James Serpell, Jonathan Silk, Richard Southwood, the Swedish Embassy, Herbert Terrace, John Treherne, and Ronnie Wallace.

I would also like to thank José Beer for editing and typing the manuscript, Judith Smith for correcting my orthography, and Janet Moult for checking references.

My thanks are due to the following:
Econ-Verlag, Vienna; Eric Hosking; the Musée Historique Lorrain, Nancy; the Musée du Louvre; Tim Page; Robin Smith Photography; the Tate Gallery for permission to reproduce photographs, and to any copyright-owners of photographs whom it has not been possible to trace.

Peterborough   M.R.
April 1986

CONTENTS

PART I

THE ROMANES LECTURE: ANIMALS AND MAN

Jewish tradition suggests we die twice. Firstly when our breathing and our pulses stop, secondly when no one remembers us. Lectures which bear a man's name usually reflect an attempt on the part of those who loved and admired him to keep his memory green. Such commendable efforts to cheat death a little are usually signal failures, for the Lecture itself acquires a name but the bearer of that name is, himself, completely forgotten. I have not yet come across a student who has listened to, and sometimes enjoyed a Romanes lecture, who knew who Romanes was (perhaps a South American Admiral who lost the Falkland Islands?). Those of us who do know, belong to a modest, rather dim band of biologists who have read his books on Animal Intelligence and Physiological Selection. But they are unlikely to have heard of a Romanes lecture or to have read his amazing poetry.[96]

Look carefully at a portrait of George John Romanes.* Are you not immediately aware that here is a fine man—representing all that was best and brightest in Victorian England? Everyone who put pen to paper concerning Romanes used such phrases as selfless devotion, transparent shining honesty, overflowing charity, tireless searcher-after-truth, essential goodness. He was, in fact, the epitome of nineteenth-century excellence, and a certain type which has long since disappeared—the amateur scientist, the philosophical naturalist—a man of means, who set up his own laboratory at home and devoted his life to an enthusiastic, passionately sincere quest for Truth. Furthermore, a man who suffered long drawn-out agonies of mind and spirit because the theory of natural selection—in which he had come to believe implicitly—had destroyed his religious faith.[93] 'I am not ashamed to confess,' he wrote, 'that with this virtual negation of God, the Universe to me has lost its soul of loveliness.'

* Details of his life throughout this lecture are based on *The life and letters of George John Romanes* by his widow.[93]

3

George John Romanes. He 'bore the white flower of a blameless life'. He was also passionately fond of shooting game birds. (Photograph by Elliott & Fry in *The Life and Letters of George John Romanes* 1896.)

Romanes never went to school—apart from a brief spell at a Canadian kindergarten and one term in a London preparatory school. He received a haphazard and aimless education at home, described later by his wife[93] as a shockingly idle and happy childhood. For the son of a Scottish Professor of Greek this was odd, but then his father regarded him as a dunce. He learned his natural history and great love of animals, roaming through the countryside, and displaying, as a boy, lack of intellectual promise and a singularly pure, unselfish, and tender nature. It is a curious fact that those zoologists who have not had the love of nature knocked out of them by the pedagogues—a process known as disciplining the mind—all share certain traits. This applies not only to Romanes but to the lesser fry I have known, such as the late Professor Howard Hinton, illiterate at fourteen years[99] who only discovered when he learned to read at the University that the Mexican snakes he took to bed with him were deadly; and the second Lord Rothschild[101] who couldn't spell or write the King's English, who tamed untameable zebras, harnessed them and drove them down Piccadilly, and assembled a collection of two and a quarter million Lepidoptera, 300 000 bird skins, and 240 000 bird's eggs. All these zoologists were imbued with an ebullient love of nature, a boyish, almost naïve delight in animals and plants which never deserted them, a boundless curiosity about natural history—and an eager-beaver mentality which made every day exciting, and drove them on to more and more collecting and experimenting.

This common denominator of the amateur scientist is so striking that one pauses—puzzled. When children have passed the imprinting stage, do they enter into another phase—which for want of better words I will call 'the acceptancy phase'—lasting well into their teens? During this period it would seem they are not merely geared to accept authority and instruction—ready for brainwashing—as suggested by the late Conrad Waddington[116]—but they accept what they find in their environment as the normal and rightful reality, so that forever afterwards they take that state of affairs as their unconscious yardstick. If, at the age of twelve, the pound (£) contains 20 shillings, notwithstanding subsequent changes like the advent of the metric system and inflation, a pound will, for them, 'really' contain 20 shillings. I will not labour the point: if you can cast back your mind to your early teens you will probably recognize some lifelong conviction, be it a religious belief or a view about lady's stockings, dating from that period. It would appear that to idle your schooldays away bird's-nesting or catching butterflies on the Scottish hills, or in the Mexican countryside or along the Chiltern escarpment, destines you for a very delightful and fruitful life-style. If only the pedagogues were such inspired mentors as trees and animals! What a different world we would enjoy. That unfortunate man Job has already suggested this: 'Who teacheth us more than the beasts of the earth or maketh us wiser than the fowls of heaven?'

Romanes began his career at Cambridge by winning the Burney Prize for an essay on Christian Prayers and General Laws, and it was not until he graduated in Natural Science that he finally gave up his intention of taking Holy Orders. After a bout of typhoid fever he also abandoned the idea of a profession and resolved to devote himself to scientific re-search, living at home with his widowed mother and sisters. He was only twenty-four when he made the decision to leave the Cambridge laboratories. At this moment a letter he wrote to *Nature* attracted the attention of no less a person than Charles Darwin who, we are told, highly appreciated Romanes' brilliant intellectual qualities and invited him 'to call'. When he walked in, Darwin held out both his hands and exclaimed, 'How glad I am you are so young'.

Curiously enough, although they belonged to a different generation, and their friendship resembled an idealized father and son relationship, both men shared several traits besides their love for one another. Both were affluent, both were devoted family men with loving and doting wives and affectionate children, both began their careers as would-be parsons and then temporarily followed some desultory medical studies.[23, 93] Eventually both became non-professional work-at-home naturalists. Furthermore both enjoyed bad health. But Romanes, in fact, died at the early age of forty-six. Darwin's qualities enumerated by Huxley[60] were almost identical with those described for Romanes by his biographers. What struck all their friends and acquaintances was their extraordinary modesty, their tireless striving after truth, and their shining goodness—both 'bore the white flower of a blameless life'.

But they shared something else in common. They were passionately fond of shooting live animals.[23] George Romanes was described as a crack shot and an ardent sportsman. His father, although mildly disapproving, hired a beautiful property overlooking the Cromarty Firth in order 'that George should have some shooting' and, according to his widow, up to his fatal illness he 'never failed to keep August 12th and September 1st in the proper way'.[93]

He took his children, aged ten, nine, and six, out shooting with him, and they never forgot the joy and pride when a bird fell, for they felt 'they had been helping their father slay the partridges'.

Darwin himself described his own passion thus: 'The autumns were devoted to shooting . . . My zeal was so great that I used to place my shooting boots open by my bedside. . . I kept an exact record of every bird I shot throughout the whole season . . . How I did enjoy shooting.' But, unlike Romanes, he had twinges of conscience about the waste of his time, for he wrote, 'I think I must have been half consciously ashamed of my zeal, for I tried to persuade myself that shooting was almost an intellectual employment; it required so much skill to judge where to find most game and to hunt the dogs well.'[23]

Yet this was the man of whom his son wrote, 'My father had the strongest feelings with regard to suffering, both in man and beast. It was indeed one of the strongest feelings in his nature and was exemplified in matters small and great— in his sympathy with the educational miseries of dancing dogs. . .'[23]

This joy in killing and inevitably maiming, causing pain and suffering, and, not infrequently, a lingering death, seems extraordinary—especially in the presence of small children whom Romanes described in his maudlin poetry as 'lambs of God'. It did not seem to conflict, like natural selection, with the Universe's 'soul of loveliness'.

Kenneth Clark[17] once described hunting as a ritual display of surplus energy and courage. 'However much one loves animals one cannot altogether regret hunting—it has given vent to so much that has enhanced the quality of human life.' Perhaps the Roman ladies who watched the gladiators slaughter 7000 wild animals in one afternoon thought and felt likewise.[15] Alister Hardy[49] explains it as a sort of built-in gene for hunting—catching one's dinner*—and one must not forget that, for thousands of years, nature was seen as a terrifying, competitive struggle. Also, remembering the 'acceptancy period', the 1850s was a period when it was the 'in thing' for a gentleman to carry a gun and arouse admiration by skilled marksmanship—in fact a class symbol and evidence of manly virtues. 'Image of war,' wrote one of our poets, 'without its guilt . . .'

But man's extraordinary ambivalence where animals are concerned—illustrated so well by Romanes and Darwin—produces an almost schizophrenic predicament in us today. We are captives of the genes which enabled us to survive in a prehistoric, hostile world,† and bedevilled by the machinations of a subconscious mind. We are the victims of our imperative drive for superiority and yet we have a need for the animal world which we are continually destroying.

The Egyptians from the first Historic and Dynastic Period onwards worshipped animals.[63] The most famous of the Gods at this time was the revered falcon Horus. But from the First to the Thirtieth Dynasty, a span of 4000 years, a wide variety of animal gods were worshipped. They included the sacred bull Apis, the ram and goose, the cat goddess; and many minor deities, the jackal, the cobra goddess, the cow goddess (The Golden One), fish goddess, scarab beetle god, a scorpion goddess; a god of storm and violence identified with many animals including pig, ass, okapi, and hippo; a crocodile god, an ibis-headed god—the ape as well as the ibis being sacred to him—a frog goddess, and so forth.

The worship of these divers deities precipitated the Egyptians into what seems to us an unhappy, ambivalent situation, for it involved them in countless animal sacrifices—their

---

* The question from first to last' wrote Joseph Campbell in *The way of the animal powers*,[13] 'was not "To be, or not to be?" but "to eat, or to be eaten?"''

† Joseph Campbell[13] points out that hardly could a contrast be greater than that between the primitive worlds of the people of the jungle and the plains. The latter depended on killing animals for their livelihood, and were dominated by an enduring sense of tension of opposites—hunter and hunted—whereas the forest dwellers were largely sustained by the vegetal abundance into which they entered with a sense of accord, and of which the animals were a natural part.

The Sacred Bull has had a longer spell as a Divine Being than Christ. (The Bull Apis (XXVI dynasty), Louvre, Paris. Reproduced in *Animals in Art* 1959.)

altars were streaming with blood. In order to satisfy, please, and appease their gods, domestic animals such as cows and geese had to be reared on a prodigious scale. But they protected their wild fauna, for they truly loved animals. The punishment for killing a falcon, whether by accident or deliberately, was death. Today in the United Kingdom the punishment for killing or capturing a peregrine falcon is a fine of £1 000. But since an Arab sheikh recently paid £260 000 for a live peregrine falcon, the fine is scarcely appropriate.

The Sacred Bull Apis, because he contained the Soul of God and was worshipped as God, could not be allowed to die of old age, but was ceremonially drowned and the flesh was probably eaten at a ritual feast (for the Egyptians were great meat eaters). Then his skin and bones were mummified and buried with royal honours in a stone sarcophagus. Apis had a longer spell as a divine being than Christ has enjoyed to date—although for obvious reasons he was frequently re-born.*

We are told in the British Museum's *Introduction to Ancient Egypt*[63] that the great number of these Gods suggests that Egyptian thinking in religious matters was haphazard and confused, but proliferation of Gods was prompted by political considerations. Similarly the Lord's pronouncement in Genesis, when He blessed Noah and his sons and said, 'The fear of you and the dread of you shall be upon every beast of the earth and upon every bird of the air, upon everything that creeps on the ground and all the fish of the sea—into your hands they are delivered'—which has been described as 'a ghastly, calamitous text'[108]—was also, probably, political. For at this perilous stage of the Israelites' history their leaders must have considered it imperative to demote the Egyptian animal gods in general and the Golden Bull in particular.

Cardinal Newman, presenting the Catholic Church's point of view[92] said, 'We in our turn have no duties towards the brute creation. Of course we are bound not to treat them ill, for cruelty is an offence against the Holy Law . . . but they can claim nothing at our hands. Into our hands are they absolutely delivered. We may use them, we may destroy them at our pleasure . . . though not our wanton pleasure.'

Pius IX refused to allow the formation of a Society for the Prevention of Cruelty to Animals in Rome[108] because this would imply that human beings had duties towards animals. The *New Catholic Encyclopaedia* states baldly that

---

* The re-born Apis was selected by the presence of special markings and patterns on his coat and skin.

experimentation on living animals is 'lawful and good', even though animals may suffer severe pain in the process.

The Medawars,[77] like the Christian Church, took the 'calamitous text' in Genesis rather literally, and suggest that Jehovah did not encourage compassion for animals. But the Jewish rabbis who, via the Talmud, subsequently interpreted the Bible, strove to rectify this impression. God, they taught, ordered kindness and consideration to animals and 'showed mercy in all his works' (Psalm 145). 'A righteous man understands the soul of his animals' we are told in Proverbs (12:10), and animals were always to be fed before the owner and his household took their own meal (Deuteronomy 11:14). Assistance must be rendered [even] to one's enemy's beast of burden which was overloaded and was lying under its load (Exodus 23:5). Man, Ecclesiastes tells us (3:18), has no pre-eminence over beasts, and Isaiah condemned animal sacrifice. To kill, or harm, or torment animals by the chase was forbidden by law, and Rabbi Meir of Rothenburg (1220)[65] went so far as to declare that any Jew who hunted with bloodhounds would forfeit life in the future world. Even the flea was spared on the Sabbath.

The rabbis tried their best, but they were not very successful. The western world seems to have accepted God's lack of compassion for the animal kingdom, and for the next 2000 years has lived up to this version of the Image most successfully.

The philosopher Descartes[27]—whose view that animals were automata, gained widespread credence—nailed his wife's pet dog to a board by its four paws and dissected it alive.[97] His wife, by the way, then left him.

Freud[40] would have told us that Descartes was, emotionally speaking, dissecting his mother.* Further he would have added that man does not like to recognize that his cruelty, sadism, love, fear, hate, reverence, and other feelings towards animals are totemism, attitudes which stem from an unconscious displacement from a human object.

But it is unnecessary to get bogged down in the subconscious since there is plenty to marvel at in the conscious

---

* Recently an interesting book[70] *The Old Brown Dog* has appeared discussing this aspect of sadism.

The Rabbis tried their best . . . . (Talmundschüler, Israel. Photograph by Cornell Capa in *Die Welt der Photographie* 1962.)

world. Some children, for instance, are notoriously cruel. In the days when public executions took place in England, youths burned live cats so that their shrieks of agony added to the general jollification.

Even the flea was spared on the Sabbath. ('La femme à la puce' by Georges de la Tour, Musée Historique Lorrain, Nancy.)

In Elizabethan times skinning frogs alive to see how far they could jump when flayed was also rated great fun by young boys. We do not know if Queen Elizabeth I disapproved or approved of this particular sport. She herself

Descartes was concerned about his soul.... He nailed his wife's pet dog to a board and dissected it alive. (René Descartes by Frans Hals.)

greatly enjoyed shooting deer with a crossbow and they were herded into her presence for this purpose.[115]

Another boyish amusement at that period was to thrust a needle through the heart of a hen to see how long it would survive. Incidentally this category of curiosity is not unknown today, for childish traits can be prolonged into manhood. A highly respected scientist caught and confined wild birds in a cage, together with poisonous insects, and watched to see if they would starve to death or venture to eat the insects. They starved to death. I think Darwin would have called this damnable curiosity.[20]

At country fairs a perennial adult amusement was biting off the head of living rats[15] and hens. Indian Maharajahs, for the sake of their ideal of beauty, enucleated the eyes of living horses and replaced them with jewels.[78] Some of you may shudder at the thought, but if you use eye-shadow or after-shave lotion you should reflect on the Draize eye test.[108] Are you in any way less culpable than the Maharajahs? Last year 18 000 experiments were performed on living animals because, we are told, the public demand safe cosmetics and toiletries.[38] You may think enough brands of toilet soap, and lipsticks, and lotions for producing a sexually attractive complexion, or concealing the odour of sweat, are already available. It is totally unnecessary to cause pain and misery to animals in order to satisfy our craving for novelty or to produce new, unnatural, 'sexy' scents.

Let us consider another facet of our schizoid society. Every year—with a peak about Christmas time, the season of goodwill on earth—no less than thirteen and a half million pet dogs and cats are turned out on the streets of American towns to die of starvation or to be put down by the appropriate authority or assigned for laboratory experiments.[83] For the same reason 100 000 are killed here in the UK.

Now let me turn to a more attractive side of our split personalities—some of the animal lovers of the world.

I will not dwell on Leda—for you know her story too well—but it should not be forgotten that Greek mythology abounds with sexual unions between human beings and animals, often gods disguised as animals.

Menninger[78] tells us that among the Sedang Moi of Indochina the legend goes that everyone was drowned in the Deluge except a woman and a dog who then cohabited and produced children. To this day, writes Menninger, Sedang women are forbidden to eat the flesh of dogs 'because they are our husbands'.

Passing sexual relations with animals are not infrequent in rural communities today.[69] One little girl, about eight years old, was found by her mother earnestly masturbating her female dog. Asked quietly what she was doing, the child answered simply 'I am trying to be nice to her'.

The Kalapalo Indians of Central Brazil[5] keep various

Christmas—Peace and Goodwill on Earth, when hundreds of thousands of unwanted dogs are turned out on the streets to die. (Christmas card by Annette.)

mammals and birds as pets, and treat them as children and
valued members of the family. These animals are never killed
or eaten. The birds are buried in special cemeteries, and their
souls, according to the Indians, live on in a bird's paradise.

16

The aborigines of Western Australia[37] also treated their dingoes as important members of their family. They were constantly caressed, never struck, only scolded verbally, and so beloved, according to an observant diarist, that their masters ate their fleas and then kissed them on the snout.[75] Dingoes, incidentally, are thought to have reached Australia from India about five thousand years ago. They are, relatively speaking, newcomers, for dogs in the Middle East have been domesticated for twelve thousand years.[13]

Of the world religions, Jainism[61] has been kindest to animals for it utterly prohibits violence and killing of any sort. Only fruit and vegetables are eaten, and in the case of plants, the leaves, never the root. Jainists were responsible for the spread of vegetarianism on the Indian continent. Their monks wear face masks to prevent tiny airborne animals accidentally perishing when they breathe.

It is fashionable to take the gilt off the Jainists' gingerbread by insisting their attitude was and is a negative variety, that is to say ahisma[78] —an avoidance of sin rather than positive kindness. A little ahisma in the western world would be of great benefit to us all.

The dismal record of Christianity where animals are concerned is mellowed by Saint Francis, a shining exception and one of the greatest amateur naturalists of all time. His enthusiasm for the natural world suggested to Singer[108] that he lived in a state of permanent jubilation and ecstasy engendered by animals and flowers. But, like Romanes, his great love for oxen and birds did not prevent him eating them.

I mentioned Queen Elizabeth I as a fine shot with the crossbow. We must not forget her cousin, Mary, Queen of Scots—a true animal lover—who, as we all know, took her poor little dog, trotting along concealed beneath her skirts, to the scaffold with her.[109]

Talking of executions reminds me of Giordano Bruno[108] who was burnt at the stake for insisting that man was in no way superior to the ant. Faced with the fire, he would not recant.

Nor should we forget the Oxford scientist who directed that his ashes should be scattered over his dog's grave.

I will not weary you with stories about the people who

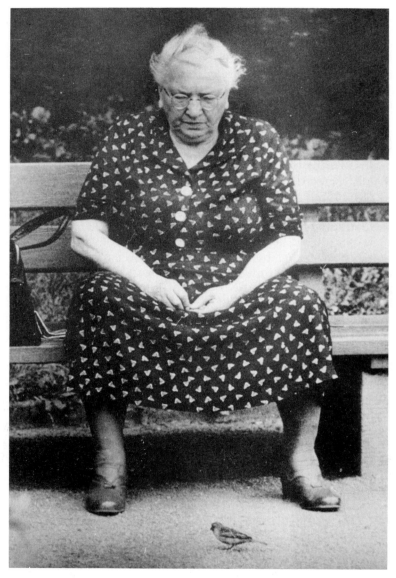

Caring is good for you. (Photograph by Ernst Herb in 'Photographic Year Book' 1958.)

have risked their lives to save their animals, or those who have bequeathed them large fortunes in their wills, nor the eccentrics who have elevated their pets to high office.* I will just draw your attention to one more fact: in the nine largest countries of the European Economic Community today there are forty-eight million animal lovers who keep dogs or cats. Another twenty-six million own pet birds. But the British are no longer the great dog lovers of Europe. The French† outnumber us by almost two to one.[80] But let me return from this schizophrenic situation to the era of Darwin and Romanes.

It dawned on naturalist philosophers about one hundred and twenty years ago that there are at least two types of evolution operating where man is concerned—one of which Alfred Wallace[117] described as 'The rapid advancement of mental organisation'. This has freed us, up to a point, from the straitjacket of natural selection by giving us some independence from our environment. In Julian Huxley's words, 'Man's ability to formulate his experience in generalized statements and scientific laws means he possesses what amounts to a second mechanism of heredity'[59]—the ability, if you like, to pass on acquired information—what the media would caption 'from loincloth to moon boots'.

Of course this type of evolution—passing on acquired information—exists for other species, but its manifestations pass unnoticed unless they are somehow related to ourselves. We noticed the bright ideas of tits only because they suddenly learned to open the milk bottles left on our doorsteps and swiped the cream off the top of our milk.[36] Now this habit may in time improve the tits' chances of survival, but it spread so rapidly across Western Europe (indoctrinating Norwegian jays on the way) that natural selection could not

---

* There is another curious aspect of our relationship with animals and that is the one-sided emphasis we place on the dog and cat characteristics, whereas we ignore our own from their viewpoint. What is attractive about us for the animals we own? There is a well-worn joke about a man who takes his horse to see his analyst and explains apologetically '. . . you see, my wife thinks she's a horse'. But there is a dearth of jokes about horses mistaking teenage girls for their mothers.

† Incidentally Paris has produced one type of dog with a very special temperament: it rides on the box seat of taxi cabs beside its master. It is alert, cocky, self-confident, interested in everything, slightly too stout and humorous.

have been involved. There just was not time. (A very amusing local variation of this new tit craze occurred: the tits in Littlehampton formed little flocks and followed the milk carts around, raiding them while the milkman was delivering to each household. Apparently they found it more profitable than flying to the individual doorsteps.)

You will appreciate that this is a bird-version of Julian Huxley's psycho-social phase of evolution* which is enormously highly developed in man and perhaps fatally speeded up, owing to our possession of language and thought. Richard Dawkins[26] coined a noun for a unit of cultural transmission, floating around within this sea of culture—a unit of imitation—and called it a *meme*. It would seem that our new attitude about animal relationships and the sharpening of our collective conscience about animals and especially a new willingness to face up to what I will call the animal schizophrenics, has all the ingredients of a successful meme. We are about to experience a fundamental change in animal—man relationship.

Plutarch was a vegetarian, and for the same reasons that I am a vegetarian. You may recall that he preferred not to chew the sores and wounds of others. So it is safe to say this meme (like the odd melanic peppered moth in the early nineteenth century, if you want a classical Oxford-generated genetic analogy[68]) has been present in low concentrations for a long time. Even as late as 1977 Kenneth Clark—who, I suspect, enjoyed a rare steak—referred to Leonardo da Vinci, on account of his vegetarianism, as 'one of an inconvenient minority', and added that he showed a consistency rare among animal lovers today. Well, in the course of only seven years this comment has become outdated. Today vegetarians are not rare, they are commonplace. There are ten million animal-loving vegetarians in the USA[66] and approximately 1.1 million in the UK (personal communication). This is not negligible, although meme evolution in this case—despite

---

* After the lecture it was pointed out to me that tits opening milk bottles[56] was a dubious example of cultural transmission, although various secondary sources (such as Alister Hardy, J.F. Wittenberger, R.A. Wallace, P.R. Marler) attribute the spread of milk-bottle opening to learning by observation or imitation. If the reader is interested in this problem of cultural transmission he should consult *The Evolution of Culture in Animals* by John T. Bonner.[8]

what I will call heterozygous vigour—has not been so rapid as the genetic blackening of the peppered moth. But the animal meme has had an electrifying effect on literature. A great many books have suddenly appeared dealing with animal/man relationship. And such excellent volumes as *Animal Liberation*, *Animal Rights*, *Animal Awareness*, *Animal Thinking*, *Animal Suffering*, *Our Lives with Companion Animals*,* and so forth, have flooded the bookstalls—all meme engendered. One disgruntled reader of *Nature*[43] wrote protesting that from April to November 1984 fourteen pages had been devoted to this subject and only half that number dealt with human rights from the Argentine to the Soviet Union.

Romanes opened up this field, although his intention was primarily to demonstrate the reality of evolution in the true Darwinian sense, and thus he stressed his belief that the difference between the animal brain and ours was one of degree, not kind. He passed over what he considered the theological distinction (here again one senses his personal dilemma) between man and animal, and the question whether or not the spirit of man differs from the soul of animals and whether one is immortal and the other is not. What he in fact achieved (despite the fact that scientists could not accept Romanes' interpretation of animal faculty) was the arousal of interest, especially in a general, rather than a specialist audience, both here and in the USA in animal thinking and animals as individuals. His contemporaries attributed his success 'To the unconstrained natural way in which his originality shines out'. Romanes certainly wrote in a delightfully enthusiastic and personally involved manner about animals, and his anecdotes were perspicacious—I recall I counted 3000 first person singulars in his volume on *Mental Evolution in Animals*.[95] He was an important factor in promoting the meme's message—in fact a great pioneer in human/animal relationship, notwithstanding the slaughter of the innocents and his whitewashing of the vivisectionists.

But where is the meme leading us? Vivisection is a matter for discussion, but there is no logical argument (unless

---

* See References, pp. 86–94.

pecuniary greed and gastronomic pleasure and gluttony are adequate reasons) in favour of eating flesh. Factory farming,[25,51] which includes practices like castration and dehorning as well as atrocious living conditions, transport, and the

Five thousand million chickens are reared annually for slaughter. (Photograph in *Animal Machines* 1964.)

terror of the slaughterhouse, is responsible for more animal misery than vivisection, gin traps, and field sports lumped together. Meat eating as practised here is also profoundly wasteful of our resources. If you like figures, it will thrill you to know we in the UK produce 280 million pounds of mutton a year and 50 million pounds of wool. An economist of my acquaintance showed me some convincing calculations, proving to his satisfaction that if we became a vegetarian nation we would also, within a very short time, be a solvent

In the United Kingdom we produce 280 million pounds of mutton per year. (Line drawing of sheep by Henry Moore. Reproduced in *Sheep Sketchbook* 1972.)

nation. The case for vegetarianism is, in my view, indisputable. But the fact that we have eaten animals for so long as a matter of course has necessitated distancing ourselves from them. This has further bedevilled the relationship.

For instance in Western Europe we don't eat dogs and cats because, by and large, we shrink from eating our friends.[107] Similarly the native women in New Guinea[37,110] who breastfeed pigs alongside their own babies, eat other people's pigs but not those they have suckled. Just as we have to depersonalize human opponents in wartime in order to kill them with indifference, so we have to create a void between ourselves and the animals on which we inflict pain and misery for profit—be they the victims of factory farming, or rats scalded (540 such experiments in 1981)[38] in the cause of medical progress. This depersonalizing void between ourselves and our victims is today filled with the bedlam of multiple impacts. In the days of our ape-like ancestors there was Daddy Ape and Mummy Ape and Baby Ape, and perhaps once a week in the middle distance one caught a glimpse of Another Ape. Today in Oxford, somehow, we have to

Native women in New Guinea eat other people's pigs—not those they have suckled.
(Photograph in *New Guinea* 1969.)

contend with hundreds of apes every morning. Small wonder we have ceased to be amiable figures in a landscape. How difficult it is for a busy research worker, caught up in the scientists' rat-race, to nip downstairs and visit the other rats in the animal floor in the basement. There is even less time for the rabbi to witness ritual killings in a discreetly concealed slaughterhouse.

In the relationship between the anti-vivisectionists and the scientists we can perceive offences on both sides, but I fancy the trained scientists deserve most censure. We should be sufficiently objective to avoid glaring sins of omission. Darwin and Romanes were both guilty. Darwin deliberately

24

We have to depersonalize human opponents in wartime in order to kill them with indifference. (Photograph by Tim Page in *Nam* 1983.)

ignored the adverse evidence placed before the Royal Commission on the abuse of experimental animals, and maintained in letters to foreign professors and to *The Times*[21] that in this respect British physiologists were as white as driven snow. Romanes went further. He accused the antivivisectionists of squandering valuable enthusiasm in pursuit of 'a harmless will-o-the-wisp . . .'[94]

Both these men were motivated by a sincere conviction that advances in medicine largely depend on experiments on living animals. In the interest of what seemed to them an almost sacred goal, both were prepared to slosh the whitewash around. Darwin, however, suffered from a bad consciénce. To Holmgren[22] he wrote: 'I know that physiology cannot possibly progress except by means of experiments on living animals, and I feel the deepest conviction that he who retards the progress of physiology commits a crime against mankind'. But to Ray Lankester he admitted[20] that, 'It [vivisection] is a subject which makes me sick with horror, so I will not say another word about it else I shall not sleep tonight . . .'

Recently the case for vivisection in medical research has been put forward most ably by William Paton.[87] He propounds the Research Defence Society's position[3] and has stated the case with compelling clarity. He is not only a talented writer but a marvellously skilled operator. I myself have watched, awestruck, while he dissected an anaesthetized cat. But I am bound to admit that reading through the pages of *Man and Mouse*, I too felt that—despite his lucid and well supported arguments—he had made use of the whitewash, albeit applied in a subdued manner. The dubious aspects of the problem had just been tactfully omitted or glossed over. Firstly I believe—no, at least let me be honest—I know that many experiments are performed on live animals to satisfy our thirst for knowledge. Many scientists are obsessed with the desire to get the right answer, not only to prove that their theories are correct, and to win both approbation and advancement—fame and fortune—but because the desire to 'know' is almost as compelling as the craving for a hard drug. Furthermore to the researcher himself the answer almost inevitably seems more significant than it really is. Secondly, all too few of those in authority make it clear to their classes and their pupils or their post-doctoral students, or those planning experiments, or those applying for vivisection licences, that an increase in human knowledge is not in itself a justification for experimenting on live animals. The Medawars[77] pointed out that it is difficult for scientists to retain a sense of primary obligation to the animal rather than to the experiment and the law. Rules are not enough. This is not stressed anywhere in *Man and Mouse*.

Finally in my experience the extreme violence of the militant activists has not 'reduced the willingness of scientists to come forward and explain'. We are one and all *appalled* at violence, but these lamentable outbursts have brought home to us our poor performance in just the area of 'explaining'. Furthermore I believe we are sufficiently sincere to recognize the fact that without the raucous clamour of the public *nothing at all* would have been done to improve the lot of factory farm and laboratory animals. Recently the University of California, at no less a place than Berkeley, has been fined $12 000 and ordered to correct longstanding deficiencies in its treatment of laboratory animals[11]—as the result of public indignation. Nor will this be a lone indictment. Would the number of vivisection experiments in the UK have fallen by 14 per cent in 1983, and scalding and burning experiments by 60 per cent without the public pressure and the media? I doubt that too. But the widening distribution of the meme will ensure that the numbers continue to fall.

The hope of real progress in human/animal relationships is foreshadowed by the meme's side-stepping and flowing past some eminent academic thinkers and philosophers.

Descartes was concerned about his soul and worried by the uncertainty of immortality—for the possession of a soul was the essential feature which distinguished man from brute creation. More recently philosophers have substituted the 'word'—the use of symbols—for the 'soul'. No doubt there are powerful genetic pressures to ensure that man considers himself apart and Chosen. To be one of the Chosen evidently has immense survival value, and consequently one who possesses certain characters subjected to intensive natural selection. This superiority complex has various manifestations. One of them is the plethora of unsupported pontifical pronouncements to the effect that since animals other than ourselves have no language, they lack awareness, they do not think and are not conscious. To quote just a few of these: N. Chomsky,[16] 'For the word is the sole sign and the only mark of the presence of thought.'; M. Black,[7] 'Man is the only animal that can talk. Without it [language] imagination, thought, even self-knowledge is impossible.'; C. H. Waddington,[116] 'The concept of consciousness is not applicable to anything but a language-using animal.'; S. Hampshire[46] asserts baldly that an animal 'does not have the concepts of order or any concepts at all.'

These attempts on the part of the philosophers to pin

down their own souls* has exercised a chilling effect—almost paralysis—on enquiry into man—animal relationship. It has proved nearly as destructive as Watson and Skinner's behaviourism—a sort of taboo against investigating conscious experience.[109] Skinner's so-called rigorous scientific psychology limited scientific data to behaviour which could be objectively observed, thus excluding thought, feeling, and mental events. This palsy is reflected in the fact that we can explore the moon but have made no serious attempt to investigate how animals think without language[114]—nor if they dream, although two thousand years ago Aristotle asserted that they did.[45,73,85] 'Behaviourism should be abandoned' wrote Donald Griffin,[44] 'Not so much because it belittles the value of living animals, but because it leads us to a seriously incomplete and thus misleading picture of reality.'

But the breeze of change is rustling the dead leaves. We are not only asking different questions, but we are discovering some new and curious side-effects of this relationship. The presence of a pet reduces hypertension.[57] A child's systolic and diastolic pressure drops if a dog merely enters the room. His or her heartbeat is reduced in the dentist's waiting-room if fish swimming in a tank are available as a distraction.[57] A barren woman is more likely to conceive if she acquires a dog or a cat. For inmates of a large State hospital, violence, suicides, and the amount of sedatives prescribed dropped by 50 per cent in wards where pets were provided.[67, 71]

Perhaps the most interesting investigations were those involving interspecific caring. For instance, girls who worked as kennel maids scored significantly higher marks for liking and affection for their animals, than social workers did for their human charges.[71] Most unexpectedly an average of 1:7 family members attend consultations in the veterinary

---

* Both Charles Darwin's wife and John Romanes' wife were anguished by their husbands' religious doubts. Mrs Darwin asked for certain lines to be omitted from letters quoted in his biography,[49] and Mrs Romanes stressed that shortly before he died Romanes declared: 'I have now come to see that faith is intellectually justifiable . . . It is Christianity or nothing.' But he then added, 'I as yet have not that real inward assurance; it is with me as that text says, "I am not able to look up", but I feel the service of this morning is a means of Grace.'[93]

surgery (100 million client contacts per year in the USA) compared with only 1.2–1.3 for attendances with the family doctors.[79]

Caring is good for you. We like to know that we can give pleasure in a simple, uncomplicated fashion. No doubt during 12 000 years of cohabitation with pets, natural and unnatural selection have seen to it that dogs and cats unfailingly respond to this need. Nor do I believe with the psychologists that our feelings for animals are invariably totemistic. Affection is lavished on the cat at least partially because we like its feline qualities. We also appreciate the unselfconscious grace of animals. Nor do they question us. We are accepted—gratefully—as we are. Gandhi summed this up: 'The appeal of the lower order of creation is all the more forcible because it is speechless.'[66]

There is one aspect of the rise of 'the word' which we must not overlook. Once man had developed language and abstract thought natural selection would automatically exclude telepathy from the human repertoire of communication. Language and telepathy combined would make life impossible—solitary and hopelessly dangerous. I could not stand up here today and give this talk if I could read your thoughts. But fortunately natural selection protects me—us.

Animals are not subject to the language barrier and I envisage profitable future research in this difficult area. It seems quite possible that animals have access to other animals' mental images and hidden emotions by a process lacking in ourselves. We have all noted with mild surprise that when the thought of going for a walk drifts through our minds, old Fido suddenly wakes up, stretches, and walks expectantly towards the door. Was he really asleep or was he watching through apparently closed lids for us to glance at our watches? Is he just a super Clever Hans? I wonder.

No talk of animals and Romanes is complete without an anecdote. I once was the bearer of very bad news and while I was sitting at my desk wondering how to tell my friend that his brother had just shot himself—in walked the friend unexpectedly, with his stupid old labrador gun dog waddling at his heels. I sat there totally bereft of words, with a feeling that an iron bar was fixed across my chest. Suddenly the labrador sat back on her haunches, threw back her head and began a long-drawn-out wavering, unearthly, high-pitched howl. We both looked towards her, astounded, for neither of us had ever heard this good-natured, sloppy old thing howl before. Nor had I ever heard a similar howl from any dog. Like Balaam's ass, she knew. She was aware of disaster. Perhaps when we are enormously distressed we emit a pheromone—a chemical messenger—which animals perceive and of which we are oblivious. Be that as it may—there is a dimension here which we should investigate.

Dogs may not be able to think, they may be unaware, they may not be conscious, but their sense of smell endows them with better memories than ours. In time we can forget what people look like and fail to recognize them, and the changes wrought by time muddle and defeat us. But at close quarters dogs always remember and recognize individuals. They may have eaten onions for lunch, have grown a beard or gone bald; they may be transvestites or sleepwalkers. They can't fool the dog. Animals can also differentiate between the old and the young, be it their own or other species—a sense we lack. Apparently the smell and the essence of youthfulness is very distinctive. Possibly they react to the electro-encephalogram (EEG) patterns[86] of other animals. It has been well demonstrated by Pampiglione that these patterns are different in puppies and adult dogs. Dogs can also recognize feeble-mindedness (I use this word because I cannot think of a better one) in both their own kind and in man. They ignore feeble-minded dogs and show fear and antagonism towards mentally afflicted human beings.

Scientists, to date, have failed to investigate and analyse evocative scents. The most famous passage in Proust's novel[91] describes the overwhelming flood of childhood memories which engulf the narrator when he tastes a little cake, the famous madeleine. As far as I know no-one has ever extracted a madeleine and passed it onto a gas chromatogram. But entomologists—familiar with the co-evolution of flowers and butterflies—can guess that the causative agent in this instance was vanillin—one of the most evocative and persistent smells we know, and the most usual flavouring of a classical madeleine.

Although we can just about hold our own with a gas chromatogram, we are so wretchedly endowed compared with dogs—let alone antelopes!—that we simply cannot imagine their world. It is difficult for us to realize that you can train a dog to smell out the eggs of gipsy moths two metres away. We can, however, assume that, figuratively speaking, the evocative madeleine is the tip of a very large iceberg and it is not difficult to conceive active images without the intervention of words, conjured up in the brain of dogs by evocative scents. Maybe they think in series of olfactory scent pictures and *déja vu*.

I am a long-term optimist so I am hopeful about the future of the animal meme. I do not think it will peter out but will stimulate research in new and productive ways. Nor do I think we shall have to wait for animals to talk in order that we may become vegetarians.

But of course I am a short-term pessimist. William Paton points out that if one dares to stop to consider the world one is overwhelmed by the suffering that is revealed. Schweitzer's philosophy[106] of a boundless reverence for life is one which one would like to emulate, but it calls for constant painful decisions and choices, taken with a heavy heart. Paton calls these the moral decisions of everyday life—true, but that makes them no less traumatic.

I fancy I derive some consolation from another aspect of daily life with the natural world—I share my living space with a starling roost of 75 000 birds. Very, very chatty; very, very messy, and incredibly marvellous—as they wheel in at dusk, their wings transparent against the setting sun, with synchronized turns and aerobatics which no jet pilot could hope to emulate. What I appreciate is that there they are—after a day spent I know not where, going about their starling business, and, mercifully, they do not know I exist.

Part of a 75 000 starling roost in my garden. Mercifully they do not know I exist. (Photograph by Eric Hosking.)

PART II

INTRODUCTION

It is evident that, for a long time to come, people in Europe and North America will continue to eat meat, conduct experiments on living animals, indulge in field sports and keep pets.

The object of Part II of the Romanes lecture is to suggest and discuss ways and means by which the suffering and discomfort of the animals involved in these activities, particularly on the farm and in the laboratory, can *now*, at the present moment, be lessened, and their lives generally improved. For this reason I do not propose to discuss conservation, the morality or immorality of using animals in 'military' experiments or simulated road accidents, rights and wrongs of vivisection, farm economics, zoos, whipping racehorses, experiments concerning cigarette smoking or drunkenness, vegetarianism (meat and fish), or the importance of animal life, or the question of animal rights, animal consciousness, or animal pain.

I am convinced that the instruction and teaching of children and young adults is the most significant aspect of the problem today, but it presents a formidable task. You can condition a boy—as indeed George Romanes was conditioned—to believe that killing game is a manly virtue, and shooting partridges a skill to be admired and encouraged, but you can just as easily condition him to photograph wild life and protect birds. There is little doubt that much of the cruelty meted out to the animals is not the result of deliberate sadism, a subconscious desire for power, conscious decisions concerning the welfare of the human race, the conquest of disease or simply naked greed, but of thoughtlessness, ignorance, indifference and the acceptance of the status quo, bolstered by custom, habit and tradition. That is why the task of the teacher is formidable. But improved legislation must go hand-in-hand with a change in attitude. We should aim at the positive promotion of the welfare of the animals over which we exercise power, rather than the amelioration of their unnecessary suffering.

FARMING

I was a competent milker at the age of ten and I enjoyed nothing more than working and playing in the cowsheds. Little overt cruelty—at any rate cruelty that a child would appreciate—was practised in the management of a prize pedigree dairy herd. I was, however, taught that bulls were dangerous, always untrustworthy, and sometimes evil. It never occurred to me that it was unkind to exercise an animal by walking it along the road with a pole attached to a ring in its nose. The idea did not cross my mind that the inevitable jerks on the pole must be excruciatingly painful. Like the vast majority of children I accepted the status quo without question, in the same spirit as I accepted sunrise and sunset. At the age of thirteen I made my first white-faced protest about the slaughter of newborn bull calves and shortly afterwards at the sale of culled cows—which I had grown to care for—on the open market. But the first stirrings of conscience were easily smothered. I was told that the buying and selling of animals was 'part of farming', and that surplus males must be disposed of—or one would have to abandon the finest of all professions and perhaps try banking! Moreover at this period of my life I struggled valiantly not to be what the mocking fellows on the farm called 'a Cissy' and I grew to accept the various miseries inflicted 'all in the day's work' on our animals.

It was not until I reached the age of 30* that I recovered from this well-meaning form of brainwashing and categorically banned dehorning of adult cattle, castration without a local anaesthetic, shelterless pastures, early separation of cow and calf, and long journeys in cattle trucks. Furthermore, I arranged that good old milk cows were put out to grass after a lifetime of service and not 'sent to the kennels'. On looking

* It was considerably later that I felt, for me personally, the only logical course I could follow was to become a vegetarian and farm accordingly; at the same time I gave up using cosmetics and wearing leather shoes. In fact it is a distinguishing trait of advancing years—as one's hormone balance changes and death approaches—to become more aware of suffering in general, and of animals in particular, and more averse to unnecessary killing.

back, it seems to me astonishing that I accepted the traditional methods beyond the age of thirteen. But I also had to fight my farm manager who was more stubbornly rooted in tradition than I.

Thus he firmly believed, despite all the evidence to the contrary, that the animals experienced no pain or distress when cast, slit, and emasculated. He was also obsessed with the idea that all my 'improvements'—which he called luxuries—such as cabs-on-tractors—when added together would prove too great a financial burden on the farm and I would, eventually, be forced to sell a part of my land. This he maintained was one of the depressing choices one was forced to make in this life. In a free market economy one must produce at least a reasonable profit or lose the farm. Yet, curiously enough, when castration-with-a-local for bulls over a year and cabs-on-tractors became compulsory, he accepted them without so much as a shrug. Apparently the law was different. I believe the same would apply to many reforms, now long overdue on the farm, including such matters as the transport and slaughter of animals. Legislation which curtails extreme methods is always resisted on the grounds that an increase in the cost of production will result (and with it the loss of cheap food), but I am convinced that, like the tractor cabs, the costs of such changes would be easily absorbed once factory farming as we know it was officially banned.

Although this is irrelevant to my main theme I feel it is instructive to pin-point another trivial example of the persistence of traditional learning on my own farm. I was told it was a 'fact', well authenticated, that the wood pigeons feeding in flocks on peas about six inches tall, were taking the 'leads', that is to say, the growing points, out of the plants. My farm manager illustrated the matter with a sketch of the terminal tendril. I accepted this apparently reasonable observation until quite by chance I examined the crops of fifty birds shot coming to a decoy in a pea-field, and found they were in fact eating the chickweed and other wild plants growing between the rows, and were totally ignoring the pea-leaves as well as 'leads'. At this moment in time they were actually weeding the fields! Thereafter I proved this point over and over again to my manager, who more than once shot the pealess birds himself, but he maintained it was just my 'luck'—since it was a 'fact' that pigeons on the farm took the lead out of peas—just as bulls castrated without a 'local' felt no pain.

Parallel with tradition there is the curious phenomenon of fashion. For a brief period dark brown eggs were sought after by the housewife, who was willing to pay more for them than the otherwise indistinguishable white or beige-shelled eggs. Today we have a senseless and pernicious predilection for 'white' veal rather than for veal of a normal colour. This means that calves are made anaemic by depriving them of sufficient iron in their food to keep them healthy. It is also fashionable at the present time for landowners—hereditary peers, ministers of the crown, the 'landed gentry', successful businessmen and so forth—to farm as a subsidiary enterprise, and to cultivate a professional image and at all costs to avoid the stigma of playboy farming. Thus we have the ridiculous spectacle of a wealthy landowner squeezing the last penny out of his fields and plantations, like an impoverished small-holder struggling to remain solvent, spraying every headland with herbicides, grubbing up hawthorn hedges to facilitate the path of the combine, grazing his cows behind an electric fence in a shelterless expanse of rye grass, housing his battery hens in concentration-camp cages, while he himself lives in a comfortable manor house or stately home, drives three cars and proves—with not inconsiderable skill and immense satis-faction and pride—that he grows on average four tons of milling wheat to the acre. So much for tradition and fashion. But the heart of the matter, the promotion of the welfare of farm animals is the concern of 'big business', and how much animal suffering and discomfort we, as individuals and collec-tives (that is, as local authorities or governments), will tolerate for the sake of cheap food, remunerative farming, profit, gluttony,[119] or simply ruthless greed. Ann Everton[31] sums it up well. 'It is a matter of weighing undeniable econ-omic values against equally valid social values.' Sad to say, a large number of business farmers, whether they are 'straight' meat or egg producers, or company investors, have the out-look of the affluent American plantation owners of two hundred years ago *vis-à-vis* their African slaves. A few decades hence we may look back in equal horror and disbelief at our twentieth-century factory farming. Meanwhile, many insist that the humane treatment of farm animals, like freeing the slaves, is both profoundly uneconomical and unnecessarily sentimental.

What can be done?

In the following pages I propose to itemize the basic requirements of farm animals, which, if met, would eliminate the principal cruelties and miseries which are inflicted upon them today. There is nothing new in these recommendations and their desirability is generally recognized and accepted, in theory at least. They are, with a few exceptions, banal to the point of boredom. Yet little if anything is done to relieve the present profoundly shocking state of affairs, except that excellent reports and guidelines are prepared, with some measured debates in the Houses of Parliament rounding them off, where economic, political, practical, veterinary, physiological, ethological, and legal implications are considered. For example, the excellent and important *Brambell Report*[9] published twenty years ago, although it aroused much interest has not initiated any *action* for the last two decades.* Small wonder that a deeply concerned, highly indignant public resort to violent methods—however deplorable—of exasperated protest. We are to blame. Talk. Talk. Talk. Legislation is postponed yet again. *Mañana*.

Husbandry

The *Brambell Report* says that 'In principle we disapprove of a degree of confinement of an animal which frustrates most of the major activities which make up its natural behaviour . . . An animal should at least have sufficient freedom of movement to be able without difficulty, to turn round, to groom itself, get up, lie down and stretch its limbs.' (Para. 37). These have been nicknamed the Brambell five freedoms.

The late Mrs Philip Snowdon (subsequently Lady Snowdon) told me that she had once experienced an attack of fish

---

* The Farm Animal Welfare Council is a direct 'descendant' of the *Brambell Report* (see the *Wooldridge Lecture*).[52]

allergy while travelling abroad and she considered severe itching without relief, a more destructive and debilitating experience than pain. Years later I recalled her vivid description when I myself developed a serious allergy from grooming cows. (I swelled up until I looked like an advertisement for Michelin tyres!) I shall never forget the intolerable discomfort experienced during the six weeks of necessary restraint of movement imposed on me by the condition—since scratching or rubbing aggravates the illness. One should feel deeply concerned about animals which are unable to scratch or groom owing to the confined space in which they are incarcerated. This practice is wantonly cruel.

Requirements urgently needed to improve the lives of farm animals are:

1. The Brambell 'five freedoms' for all stock, mammals and birds;
2. A well bedded, preferably dry, lying area for all stock;
3. The provision of perching and nesting boxes for all birds;
4. A diet to keep the animals in full health and vigour;
5. Access to clean drinking water for housed animals;
6. A milk substitute (or other manufactured diet) suitably reinforced with iron, should be provided for veal calves so that the animals are not deficient in this element. Palatable roughage for calves should also be provided daily, from a week after birth onwards. (*Brambell Report*. Rec. 19*.)

These minimum requirements should be imposed by regulations and the law. Every case is supported by sound scientific evidence, if indeed such support is required, to bolster commonsense and decency.

Farm buildings

Rate relief on farm buildings was introduced with a view to ameliorating hardship to animals, due to exposure and the vagaries of our climate. This does not apply to factory farms

* The Quantock loose-housed system of veal production has been recently developed by Volac which has resulted in the creation of a novel, integrated, human veal industry. It is a gloomy thought, however, that over a million 30-day calves, mostly reared in crates, were exported live from the UK in 1978–80 for further rearing in crates on the Continent. Regrettably, French chefs especially prefer white meat.

and there should be rating of all farm buildings in which animals are permanently confined.

Livestock buildings should be licensed on an annually newable basis, subject to compliance with the requirements set out above and the current *Codes of Recommendations*.[81, 82]

Stockmen should be licensed after suitable training. There should also be a law governing the ratio of stockmen to stock.

Numbers of stock

A legal limit should be set (as in Switzerland) controlling the number of stock held by any one producer or firm. In the UK today numbers have become unmanageable and it is not unusual for a single producer to have 500 000 laying hens*, or 2000 sows. A strict application of the ratio of stock to stockmen would come as an alternative solution to this patently unsatisfactory situation.

Fire

Fire and incendiaries will only affect relatively few unfortunate animals, compared with the numbers sent to slaughter. But in the UK a large proportion of cattle are housed in courts and sheds totally lacking in fire protection, despite the Ministry of Agriculture's leaflet (*701*),[81] which among other things deals with this aspect of the welfare of livestock. Cattle are at special risk owing to the inflammable nature of straw bedding and hay, and are simply roasted alive if their living quarters catch fire. Owners prefer to insure against this risk, rather than incur the expense and bother of adequate protection such as automatically opening doors, triggered by smoke or heat. Farmers are inundated with free literature and are disinclined to find the time to read, let alone obtain, *Codes of Recommendation* and will not do so until the Recommendations become enforceable Regulations. 'It is a sad fact', said Tom Cox in the House of Commons,[47] 'that the existing laws are hopelessly out of date.'

Do we laugh cynically or wring our hands?

---

* In 1950 a hen laid on average 165 eggs per annum. Twenty-five years later this had increased to 239.[54]

Transport

The majority of people in the UK today accept the fact that animals are reared to be slaughtered and eaten. However, if they were aware of the conditions in which these animals are transported and killed they would be horrified, revolted, and incensed.

Two curious facets of human nature contribute to this miserable situation. Firstly, living animals in large numbers are to some extent unattractive, or even repulsive. This applies to crowds of human beings as well as huge flocks of chickens. Handlers and stockmen lose sympathy with their charges and can deal with them callously and harshly if they are very numerous. Secondly, the owners of live stock lose interest in their beasts and birds once they are sold and have left their premises. Just as you have to distance yourself from the men you must kill in battle, so you are inclined to distance yourself from the animals you send to other people's tables. Be that as it may, it is intolerable that we have to witness cruelty on this scale. Animals should be spared the horror trips—long and arduous journeys, cramped inside small crates, and exposed to cold, wet, and often hunger and thirst, as well as fear and distress. Sending animals abroad for slaughter, so that the owners can squeeze an extra few pence out of their carcasses should be totally banned. Curiously enough many Frenchmen prefer to import live animals and then fatten them locally for fresh meat to their taste—a fact which stimulates export of our livestock.

'As an expression of the concern of the House', said Peter Griffiths,[48] '. . . we do not wish cheap food, which we all accept as desirable, to be obtained at the expense of suffering to the animals concerned'.

But we have been *forced* to accept this, because—take the case of poultry—the Council's *Report on the Welfare of Poultry at the time of Slaughter*[32] was published in January 1982, and two years and four months later the relevant Bill was still snailing through the House. If chickens had the vote, no doubt the process would have been hastened.

Slaughter

It is estimated that more than five hundred million cattle, sheep, pigs and poultry are slaughtered every year in the UK for human consumption.[103] The Farm Animal Welfare Council have produced an excellent Report on the Welfare of Livestock (Red Meat) Animals at the time of Slaughter[33] with one hundred and seventeen Recommendations. To the ordinary farmer such as myself, the recommendations appear to be pursued by the powers-that-be with gloomy inactivity. Perhaps behind the scenes there is considerable progress? Although these recommendations are rather lengthy I am reproducing them here in full (Appendix pp. 79–85). In Germany during the Hitler régime the population as a whole pleaded that they had no knowledge of the concentration camps, and this ignorance exonerated them from the sin of tacit approval. If the Council's recommendations are widely read and their significance appreciated, at least we cannot plead ignorance of the malpractices which are now current in the UK. If the housewives were compelled to visit slaughterhouses as they exist today, we would have a great many more vegetarians and the sale of sleeping pills would rise sharply.

The most important aspect of the Council's recommendations—and this applies to every aspect of farming—is the need for more inspection and supervision and more training for personnel. My own opinion is that the granting of licences should always depend on compliance with regulations. I have seen this work wonders when grants were withheld from a scientific organization until they 'toed the line' with regard, for instance, to the size of their cages and stalls, and the qualifications of their personnel. How much would this cost the taxpayer? Personally I doubt the public would object to the extra cost involved. Both in Germany and the UK non-cage eggs are more expensive than battery eggs but they are always in demand. A poll carried out by MORI for the National Farmers Union[6] in 1983 revealed that 63 per cent of the people surveyed were willing to pay more for food to improve the conditions for livestock. If proper supervision of slaughterhouses meant one meatless day a week, but less cruelty, I do not believe there would be an outcry.

Ritual killing

A further report by the Farm Animal Welfare Council[34] concerns *Shechita* and *Halal*, the methods of slaughter required by the religious beliefs and laws of Orthodox Jews and Muslims respectively. Whether or not the methods of slaughtering animals according to these religious beliefs and regulations is more cruel than our own methods—and I myself have been persuaded by scientific evidence and personal observation that it certainly is—the problem pales into relative insignificance when it is reviewed against the mass cruelty of our farm industry in general. We should not tackle one without the other. But since this question involves much wider and important issues like freedom of religious beliefs, and philosophical considerations such as imputed racial persecution, I propose to single it out for special attention.

The vague belief of the majority of English people is that the laws governing Jewish ritual killing are laid down somewhere in the Bible.* Furthermore, most so-called 'liberal' Jews have only a very superficial understanding of what is involved. If you press your aquaintances on this point they usually confess that they have either 'never thought about, or would 'rather not think about it'. Orthodox Jews, of course, follow the traditional teaching of their Rabbis unquestioningly, and accept the commands of God received via Moses, and today, from their priests.

The laws and rules governing the Jewish method of ritual killing are not laid down in the Bible, although Deuteronomy (12:15, 16) and Leviticus (17:10-12) give certain explicit directions concerning the slaughter of animals for the table. The most emphatic command concerns the consumption of blood which is sternly forbidden: 'And whatsoever man there be of the house of Israel or of the strangers that sojourn among you, that eateth any manner of blood: I will even set my face against that soul that eateth blood and will cut him off from among his people . . .' And again: 'Therefore I said unto the children of Israel. No soul of you shall eat blood . . .' In Deuteronomy (12:15-16) it is stated: 'Notwithstanding

---

* This impression is reinforced by the fact that the Chief Rabbi and Solomon Gaon[62] in their *Declaration by the Jewish Ecclesiastical Authorities of Great Britain*, state that 'the Jewish method of slaughtering animals for food, known by the Hebrew word "Shechita" is divinely ordained by the word of God as found in the Holy Scriptures.' They do not explain that they are referring not only to the text of the Scriptures, but to the subsequent interpretation or 'commentary' known as the Oral Law which is equally binding in Jewish jurisprudence.

thou mayest kill and eat flesh in all thy gates whatsoever thy soul lusteth after . . . only ye shall not eat the blood.'

Another very explicit Biblical command is that Jews themselves must not eat an animal which has died a natural death. Deuteronomy (15:21) also makes it crystal clear that an animal which has 'any blemish therein, as if it be lame or blind or have any ill blemish' must not be used as a sacrifice to God but '. . . Thou shall eat it within thy gates; the unclean and the clean person shall eat it alike . . . only thou shalt not eat the blood thereof . . .'

As it will be seen, it is the interpretation of the health, injuries, and malformations permitted and not permitted in an animal killed by Shechita for kosher meat, that is the crux of this controversy.

The rules governing the daily life of Orthodox Jews are codified in the *Shulkhan Arukh*, the work of Rabbi Joseph Caro,[14] published in 1564. This code is founded in the first place on the enactments of the *Torah* (the five books of Moses—the Pentateuch) as interpreted by the *Talmud*, a vast compilation, which is held to be largely inspired by the Oral tradition. Its composition began in the early years of the first century, and it contains the Halakha, that is, the legal and ritual mandatory rules of the *Talmud*, finally edited in the fifth century. This, in its turn, was followed by a virtually continuous series of commentaries of rabbinical scholars in various countries in the Middle Ages, on the basis of which the final code, *Shulkhan Arukh*, was established as the authoritative set of laws and enactments governing the life and observances of Orthodox Jews. This is summarized in the *Encyclopaedia Judaica*[30] as 'the legal side of Judaism, which embraces personal, social, national or international relationships and all the other practices and observances of Judaism'. This seems an accurate description.

One of the parts of the ritually slaughtered animal which according to the *Talmud* must not be injured before death is the membrane covering the brain. This is why Jewish law decrees that the animal cannot be stunned or shot or electrocuted before having its throat cut, for all these methods could injure the brain or might kill it before the knife descends. The Farm Animal Welfare Council[33] rightly (in my opinion) insists that an animal about to be slaughtered should be rendered unconscious before dying, but it suggests two methods for achieving this end—stunning or anaesthetizing.

It has been pointed out that if the former method was enforced all Orthodox Jews would be compelled to become vegetarians. This in itself is not a terrible fate. In the UK today there are five times as many voluntary vegetarians[41] as Jews. This is chiefly because (although we may have enjoyed our chicken broth and calves liver in the past) we object to the raising of animals for slaughter, and are outraged by the cruelty and misery inflicted on them in the process of rearing, transport, and death. Nor is the health of vegetarians—particularly if eggs and milk* are included in the diet—in any way inferior to that of non-vegetarians. But it is understandable that people prefer freedom of choice in such matters, particularly if they feel the decision has somehow been extorted at the expense of a religious principle.

However, the second method suggested by Richard Harrison's Committee,[33, 34] namely pre-slaughter anaesthesia, with nitrous oxide or some other inert gas, does not injure the membrane covering the brain nor render the animal sick and is completely reversible. It is patent that those of us who have had teeth removed while anaesthetized with laughing gas, wake up from our enforced and dreamless bout of unconsciousness none the worse for the experience. It is also a simple matter to ensure that no overdose is administered. Anaesthesia is neither forbidden nor accepted by the Talmudic interpretations and teaching, for the simple reason it was unknown at the time. In fact it is irrelevant to the question of ritual slaughter, which would still be taking place according to the Jewish law, just as transport of the animals by a motor lorry (unknown when the Temple was standing) is also irrelevant. Furthermore controversy concerning the Weinberg Casting Pen[34, 112] become unnecessary since an anaesthetized

---

* Providing methods of transport, housing and slaughter are improved, most of us would feel free to eat eggs and drink milk. I eat the eggs of free-range hens, and those dairy cows that have to be slaughtered are killed on the farm under the supervision of the farm manager. (Ideally, if the right supervision were to be organized, all slaughter in my opinion ought to be done on the farm.) My conscience is thus reasonably clear, although by making use of animal products I am not a true vegetarian.

animal can be turned upside down while it is unconscious without causing it stress or pain. Unfortunately stunning by violent methods, possibly leading to death or brain injury, has become confused in some peoples' minds with the question of simple unconsciousness. Both the Bible and the *Talmud* consistently urge kindness and consideration to animals and it seems that, by adopting a reversible anaesthetic prior to the act of ritual killing, the Biblical and Talmudic laws are sustained and supported rather than challenged and flouted.

In the *Harrison Report*[34] it is suggested that the law which makes stunning or anaesthetizing compulsory should be delayed for a period of two to three years. During this time further experiments could lead to perfecting the existing equipment and no doubt improving the methods of administration. At the end of this transition period I hope anaesthetizing will be made compulsory in *all* slaughterhouses in the UK, not merely in those serving Jews and Muslims. The method will certainly be available for killing chickens and turkeys, since recent research in this area has made significant progress.

THE LABORATORY

I began collecting butterflies as a young child. I thought they were beautiful, and I longed ardently to have them for myself forever. My father was a keen entomologist and he encouraged my delight in butterflies; he killed them in a cyanide bottle, set and labelled them for me. I had no clear understanding, at that time, of the difference between live and dead butterflies, I merely longed to possess them. Thus I became a collector.

A curious episode marked my sixth year. One summer afternoon I was playing in a little wood with my sister, while the nursemaid, who was instructed to keep a watchful eye on us, sat with her back to us, knitting assiduously in the shade of a beech tree. Among the dry leaves we found a toad. First we played ball with it, then we bounced it against several tree trunks and then decided to impale it on a thorn. Mercifully, at this juncture, the toad made good its escape. I remember I experienced a sense of excitement while we victimized the toad and I also recall that the plan to impale it was associated with a desire to 'see what it would do'. This, in fact, was my first scientific experiment. At bedtime, giggling, but also with a sense of mild guilt—of having been naughty—I told my parents the story of the luckless toad. I remember they were in evening dress. I now realize they were also aghast, and incredulous. The nervous nursemaid bolstered the belief that I had invented the whole story, since she assured them she had 'never taken my eyes off the little girls for a moment' and thus nothing of the sort could have occurred. My parents, still puzzled, and uneasy, hurried away to their dinner engagement.

Butterfly collecting grew apace and soon the collection became an aim in itself. I reared caterpillars and once suffered agonies of remorse because I forgot to feed them, but I experienced no pangs when popping a valuable specimen into the killing bottle. By this time the insects were not only exquisite and desirable but had become *trophies*, and also a way of winning the approbation of my father, and inflating my ego. Doubts began to creep in when I was thirteen. An ancient retired cobbler worked as a professional collector for my father and—I was now older—I began to look askance at his glass jar crammed with the common brown moths ('the Black Hole of Calcutta'). I remonstrated with my father: 'Why should Mr Holland kill all those common moths which are of no use for your collection?' 'Oh,' said my father carelessly, 'leave the old man to do it his way.' Two years later my father died. Simultaneously I discovered I no longer wanted to collect butterflies.* But my interest in natural history revived when I helped my brother fulfil his school holiday task, namely to dissect The Frog. These animals were chloroformed in a glass jar. Never for a moment did I mourn their passing. I believed this was essential in the cause of scientific learning, the acquisition of knowledge, and future scientific discoveries. The sense of wonder which I had lost when I abandoned the butterfly collection returned on examining the internal anatomy of the luckless and beautiful amphibian, and, fortunately for me, proved durable. When I eventually found my way into a laboratory, 'discovery', however trivial, took the place of the Purple Emperor butterfly of my childhood, and those who read my publications with interest—however few—took the place of my approving father. I naïvely believed in the significance of the modest research I was engaged in—for I was convinced that the discovery of new species, however obscure, and of new facts, not only increased knowledge but might lead to important advances in physiology, psychology, medicine—who knows? To me every facet of zoological research seemed interesting and exciting and I told everyone about it. I must have been a very tiresome schoolgirl.

During World War II David Lack, the most distinguished ornithologist of his day, asked me if I could shoot a few robins for him. 'Some people don't like shooting robins,' he added. I assured him that I did not mind. This was a lie. I minded very much, but I believed this was an inherent sentimental weakness in my character, which must be concealed

---

* For the accurate identification of insect species basic collections are a necessity, and I would not discourage children from collecting in moderation.

and overcome.* The fact that I remember the death of that first robin so clearly, forty years later, shows that I only succeeded with difficulty. It was a cold, windless winter day and the robin was sitting on a branch spangled with hoar frost, with his feathers fluffed out like a brown and scarlet tennis ball. I felt *terrible*.

Looking back at the first half of my life as a zoologist I am particularly impressed by one fact: none of the teachers, lecturers, or professors with whom I came into contact—and that includes my kindly father—none of the directors of laboratories where I worked, and none of my co-workers, ever discussed with me, or each other in my presence, *the ethics of zoology*. Nor did they ever ask me what I was really trying to do, what were my zoological aims and aspirations, and in what framework I saw the life-cycles I was elucidating. No one ever suggested that one should respect the lives of animals in the laboratory or that they, and not the experiments, however fascinating and instructive, were worthy of greater consideration. On one occasion I demonstrated a trematode life-cycle at a Royal Society Conversazione,[98] the first with three different hosts to be discovered in the UK. I had managed to assemble live sea birds, fish, and snails, and one could watch the larval worms, like minuscule twinkling comets, swimming towards the fish and penetrating beneath their scales. But no one asked me if my captive black-headed gulls enjoyed good health or suffered when heavily infected with ovipositing worms, or if the fish were injured by the invading cercariae.

The fact is, teacher and pupils alike—quite aside from the question of earning their livings or furthering their careers as scientists—were brainwashed and self-indoctrinated. We were on the whole a rather moral group of seekers–after–truth, who loved the natural world and who were happily convinced

---

* I know several zoologists who have admitted that they suffered from the fear of being dubbed 'unmanly' and struggled to overcome their dislike of causing animals pain, or killing them. Furthermore two or three have explained that they switched from vertebrate to invertebrate physiology because they refused to cause suffering to rats, rabbits, dogs, or cats. It should be stressed here that invertebrates should also be anaesthetized before dissection or stressful experiments. There is a tendency for people to ill-treat animals much smaller than themselves, as if reduced size made them insensible.

of the importance of our subject—our research—but who were, lamentably, disinclined to think. It took me another thirty years of natural history and zoological laboratories before I, myself, began to consider the matter seriously and allowed my doubts to crystallize. This fortunate, but traumatic experience I owe to my eldest daughter who, as a schoolgirl, resolutely marched out of her zoological classroom never to return. She refused to kill and then dissect an earthworm.

The penny dropped.

Sadism, indifference and motivation

When we are teaching, there are several awkward prospects we tend to ignore or sidestep, perhaps suppress. I have singled out three of them.

'The young' remarked Locke,[72] 'torment poor animals with a seeming kind of pleasure.' Lecturers usually dodge this issue. Apart from the fact that the subject is distasteful, it is really difficult to find a psychiatric textbook which deals adequately with the problem of sadistic cruelty. Perhaps we are all reluctant to face the ugly reality that unconscious sadism is an inherent quality of mankind. Lecturers also skirt round the embarrassing reality that cruelty and sexual arousal are often linked. Yet all zoologists should be familiar with the fleeing female and the aggressive domineering male, and, not infrequently in the animal kingdom, intercourse with a punishing pattern: the spined penis of sharks and the domestic cat[113] are obvious examples of this phenomenon.

Certain professions attract certain types of individuals and then provide the environment which promotes and reinforces just those characteristics supplying the initial impetus to become a surgeon, a zoologist, or a hairdresser as the case may be. Which of us has a psychological need for dominance and power? Is science an aggressive pursuit? Have we not outgrown the necessity of subduing Nature? We do not know, but every student should be encouraged to think about the subject and discuss it.

I was once taken aback by an unusually able assistant of mine suddenly deciding to quit zoology. Apparently she had been given a live, instead of a dead mouse, to feed to a stoat, in which we were studying pelage change. Not having the courage to kill the mouse herself, she hurriedly pushed it into the cage. She watched fascinated while the animal crouched terrified in a corner, facing the tense, bright-eyed stoat preparing for the kill. To the girl's consternation she then experienced a violent orgasm. After considering the implications of this disturbing revelation she decided she was not temperamentally suited to look after live animals. Konrad Lorenz[74] wrote rather melodramatically: 'To any man who finds it equally easy to chop up a live dog and a live lettuce I would recommend suicide at his earliest convenience.'

Lecturers addressing zoological and medical students should be at pains to direct their attention to this problem of sadism and explain that here there is something rather different from the flare of illtemper which prompts the put-upon office-boy to redirect his frustration and aggression and kick the cat downstairs.

Unless these well-concealed impulses are brought into the open and we become fully conscious of their meaning, they will continue to disturb and distort our scientific ideals.

Indifference, a blunting of the sensibilities, is perhaps a more important problem than the elimination of active sadism. It is necessary, if life is not to overwhelm us, that familiarity should breed a certain form of contempt. I, myself, was temporarily paralysed by fear during the first big air raid I experienced in World War II, and again suffered a brief period of amnesia after the Bristol blitz. Yet I eventually became quite a competent air raid warden! One can get used to anything. Indifference is just round the corner. Every scientist from the most brainy professor to the lowliest technician involved with animal experimentation should recognize this fact, discuss it, and evolve rules to counteract the effect of lack of compassion and sympathy, or however you choose to define the degree of callousness or indifference— great or small—you can expect to develop with the passage of time.

'Insensitivity to experimental animal brutalises the experimenter,' wrote Vince Dethier,[28] a scientist for whom I have boundless admiration. 'The experimenter should assume that the animal feels and should therefore make every effort to forestall pain. This is one thing about animal experimentation of which I feel certain.'

Michael Balls[4] describes an extreme case of such brutalization in a laboratory in the USA where, for instance, the dental cement used to fix helmets on the heads of baboons prior to being subjected to non-impact head injury was removed with a hammer and screwdriver; this required a number of blows; the operators were careless, and on one occasion sliced off the animal's ears by mistake. This was only one example of the events which shocked and revolted him.

There will always be, as Robert Hinde[55] pointed out, a grey area between legislation and practice where experiments are performed on live animals, and in this sphere a scientist's conscience must operate. Eduction and revised legislation together can help us overcome the subconscious and conscious pitfalls, licensed sadism, totemism, lapses, rationalizations—or just being in a hurry—which may beset our moral faculties at such times.

Motivation is also a matter which deserves careful consideration and scrutiny. Fame and fortune have to be balanced against the animals exploited in the process of conducting the experiments. In other words one must be wary of the scientific ambitions which can act against the interests of the animal object. The legitimacy of an experiment, says Robert Hinde,[55] must be determined by assessing the probable gains to knowledge. But this cannot be measured. The assessment is left to us. At one time I believed that an increase in knowledge was in itself a justification for experiments on live laboratory mice. I did not ask myself if this new knowledge was really necessary, or would be of obvious benefit to mankind, rather than a nebulous possibility. Here are two concrete examples. I had discovered a very potent toxin, new to science, in a species of moth. To investigate its potential—whether it was carcinogenic, or suppressed tumours, or affected nerve tissue, or interfered with circulation or the function of the brain and so forth, my collaborator and I injected an extract, via the intra-peritoneal route, into live mice. After ten hours the mice died from massive internal bleeding. Today, in retrospect, I can still recognize the potential interest of this new toxin, but I see no justification whatsoever—particularly at this stage of the work—for inflicting pain and misery on a living animal in order to learn more about the substance in question. First of all my own interest and enthusiasm exaggerated the importance of this discovery. Secondly, I accepted what was a conventional test in our laboratory without question and without careful assessment of the possibly distressing effect on the mice. Thirdly, I did not enquire into alternative methods of testing the toxin. Eventually I came to my senses and began to consider the implications of this line of research more coolly and carefully, and in fact found that our extracts could be tested on *in vitro* preparations, that is, on isolated animal tissues, like lines of cells, or organs isolated in the course of medical instruction, and obtained easily after the animal concerned has died. These tests were inferior, since they were far less informative, but I judged they were nevertheless, at that stage of the investigation, adequate for the purpose.

On the other occasion I asked the late Geoffrey Harris if he thought rat fleas required the influence of the host's sex hormones in order to breed successfully—like the rabbit flea we had recently investigated. He immediately suggested hypophysectomizing a rat, and, if the fleas bred on such an animal, it would prove they were not hormone dependent. I agreed. In retrospect I find it disquieting that I did not question his proposal to remove part of a rat's brain in order to prove the rat fleas' dependence on host hormones. I would *now* give the rat the benefit of the doubt, and, if necessary, leave the question unanswered. Harris was a man for whom I had immense admiration and respect. Sadly, only death deprived him of a Nobel Prize. The climate has now changed—but I wonder if he would have made a similar suggestion today.

These are two relatively trivial examples (but not for the rat or mouse) of where the conscience of the scientists must operate. It is so easy to kid oneself into believing the work is more significant than it is (the ego so easily triumphs) and, who can tell, lead on to some dazzling discovery. Maybe you are not a good scientist unless you believe just that—and therefore you require the restraint and the additional prop of legislation. As William Paton[87] pointed out, in life one is constantly confronted with painful alternatives and difficult choices, but at least in the laboratory it is necessary to remind oneself constantly that a primary obligation is owed to the animal, not the experiment.

Painkillers and sedatives

One of the strangest and most unfortunate lacunae in the teaching of zoology, physiology and animal psychology is the lack of interest and training in pain-associated and pain-relieving pharmacology. This should be a carefully thought-out, up to date, and strongly emphasized part of every degree course. Many postgraduates who have specialized in these subjects, subsequently become involved in experiments with live animals. The lack of interest and casual—if not callous— disregard of this serious aspect of animal experimentation leads me to be more specific in the following paragraphs than in other parts of this book.

Today there is a wide variety of sedatives and analgesics available for use with both small and large animals. They are safe and simple to administer, have a broad therapeutic index, and are highly effective. They should be widely and generously used, not only in justifiable scientific vivisections, which cause pain and terror by manipulation and surgery, but on farm animals—for example, for de-horning, castration, and difficult deliveries.

A period of 5–30 minutes total comatose, insensitive anaesthesia can be induced by administration via the intravenous or intraperitoneal route; this normally provides ample time in which to perform most procedures, and avoids the hassle otherwise generated. More important still, it avoids the animal's fear and pain; incidentally, the lack of struggle and tension allows the experimenter or operator to perform a more deft, rapid, and less traumatic job.

There is no excuse in 1986 for any experimental animal to suffer undue pain and terror. This applies equally to post-operative situations, as well as immediately before or during the operations themselves.

Ketamine hydrochloride, recently introduced (Ketoset Injection; C-Vet Ltd., Suffolk, UK) is an excellent drug for inducing anaesthesia with associated amnesia and analgesia in cats, dogs, and laboratory animals. It also works well in the case of non-human primates, where fear is perhaps a more significant factor than anything else in the context of unnecessary suffering and cruelty.

In larger animals such as the sheep, goat, pig, cow, and horse, a single intravenous injection of pentobarbitone sodium (Pentothal; May and Baker Ltd., Essex, UK) will simply induce a rapid short-duration anaesthesia (for 10–20 minutes) with an equally rapid and uncomplicated recovery. It is said that a mild barbiturate-induced depression may occur over the next 6–12 hours, but I have never experienced this myself (16 trials).

An even newer and better method for large animals, though slightly more complex to administer, is the combination of two drugs; slow intravenous introduction of the tranquillizer zylazine (Rompun; Bayer UK Ltd., Suffolk, UK) followed two minutes later by a single intravenous injection of ketamine hydrochloride. This induces complete, deep anaesthesia for 10–20 minutes. The animal then wakes up and stands up suddenly and will continue feeding as if nothing has happened.

The cost of Rompun, I was told, is 'the only real drawback'. This is a question of priorities. The time has come, I believe, when expensive painkillers will be accepted and economies made, if need be, in other areas. Unfortunately, many farmers and laboratories have a distorted view of priorities in this context.

Where full recumbent anaesthesia is undesirable, sedation with analgesics is the best solution. A whole range of very effective compounds are available, including Rompun and acepromazine maleate (ACP; C-Vet Ltd., Suffolk, UK). Given either intravenously or intramuscularly they provide a variable level of sedation that persists for 20–45 minutes. The treated animal appears to slip off on a 'carefree trip' so that fear of human intervention disappears. A newer and quite miraculous drug developed in Finland is called dometodine hydrochloride (Domosedan; Farmos Group Ltd., Finland). It has a tremendously wide margin of safety. Only 0.75 ml of this material injected intravenously into a 16-hand horse will, within 2–3 minutes, induce complete sedation with a high degree of analgesia. The treated animal stands with closed eyes for about 20 minutes and seems to be 'dreaming of pleasant green pastures'. On waking, it yawns and continues with daily life as if nothing had happened. While under the influence of the drug, pain response is greatly reduced and such operations as wound suturing and castration can be carried out with ease. The horse barely notices what is happening to it and any fear it manifested previously totally abates. When the 'patient' is thus relaxed—as with total anaesthesia—the experimenter/operator also works more efficiently.

The long-term suppression of pain following surgery is one that requires far more thought and concern. The old stand-bys, morphine and pethidine, could be used much more widely and routinely in small and large animals. There is a curious and, to you and me, *incomprehensible* reluctance, on the part of people who have permission to administer pain-relieving drugs, to do so. My doctor, who died of cancer, told me that when his father was dying of the same disease he used to sneak in and give old Dad an adequate shot, because his own doctor was so unnecessarily parsimonious with the painkiller. I can, unfortunately, cap this story several times over, but where animals are concerned, this ghastly syndrome is even more acute, especially if the experiment concerned has been a failure and the animal is dying of, say, some infection following the operation.

Apart from morphine, there is a more modern adjunct, the prostaglandin synthetase suppressing drugs such as miclofenamic acid (Arquel; Parke-Davis Ltd. Gwent, UK), and phenylbutazone (Phenyzone; C-Vet Ltd., Suffolk, UK) which are a tremendous help. They (and many others) greatly reduce the inflammatory process in the body, thereby reducing swelling with its associated pain and misery. These drugs are cheap, harmless, and effective. They should be used in any situation that is accompanied by long-term pain.

Today, the average student in zoology and animal psychology knows little or nothing of all this; he has not been taught to think about pharmacology and has not the slightest idea how these drugs are made and how they act. Such a student also has no understanding, insight, or knowledge of pain, apart from meagre personal experience. He or she may eventually be quite prepared to carry out experiments on animals, steeped in ignorance of this vital aspect of their work. It is a well-known fact that we soon forget pain. If we could really recall the misery of toothache or the last hour of child birth we would find daily life too difficult. This may account for some of our indifference to animal suffering. But the scientist in the laboratory has no excuse. Knowledge can overcome this lamentable, protective lack of insight.

What can be done?

The single most consequential factor to ensure 'a better deal' for laboratory animals is a practical change in priorities. Every student should be imbued with the idea that the welfare of the animals is of primary importance. This is essential for any zoologist or physiologist worth their salt. Today, few heads of departments take a personal interest in either the welfare of the animals kept on their premises, or in their ultimate fate, especially when experiments are written-off as failures. Protests about the treatment of laboratory animals almost invariably stem from grass roots—the students, not from their mentors, least of all from the top.

I have regretfully accepted the necessity for using living animals in experiments, because I believe certain advances in medical and veterinary science and physiology, from transplants to vaccines, depend to a greater or lesser extent on this type of investigation. (This does not mean I evade the unpleasant fact that these animals are sacrificed for us.) It follows that I also believe such a view must be held by any head of a medical, zoological, or physiological laboratory. But the reluctance of heads of departments to assume their responsibilities in this area stems from the fact that, basically, keeping animals for experimentation is an unpleasant task. It may not be consciously so, people may be hardened and practical, or sadistic, but by-and-large they shrink inwardly from inflicting pain; consequently they shy away from the whole prospect of the role that animals must play in the laboratory. Also, it is a rather boring, time-consuming occupation and there is an almost irresistible temptation to stick one's head in the sand or in a pile of forms—sometimes in the clouds—and delegate the job. The larger the establishment the greater the incentive to separate the animal house from the department, or organize things in such a way that one large animal house serves several departments. Thus the staff and the students distance themselves from the inherently disagreeable necessity of hurting and killing the animals they study and appreciate. But *if* the job has to be delegated, genuine trouble should be taken to find a deputy with the same priorities and sympathies as the head of the department.*

In a recent article in *Nature*[24] it was pointed out that in order to ensure adequate inspection of laboratories, such as those suggested by the National Institute of Health, huge sums of money are required. In the new regulations being formulated in the UK[2] it is proposed to increase the number of inspectors by 40 to 15-21 per cent. This is not a very realistic figure when the number of experiments on live animals in 1984 amounted to three and a half millions (3 497 335).[39]

Of course improved inspection is absolutely necessary and Government funding can be found, but at best it is a poor solution. The head of the department must give the animals top priority and demand a standard from students and technicians far above that which the letter and spirit of the law requires.

Further suggestions

1. Animal house technicians should be selected for different reasons than they are today. It is not enough to be trained either as a biologist or a technician. The individual's attitude to animals should be carefully evaluated; only those who are sympathetically orientated towards them should be chosen. If this suggestion could be put into practice in every animal house, it would improve the lot of laboratory animals more than any other single factor.

---

* It is hoped that the new legislation (*Animals (Scientific Procedures) Bill*)[2] will ensure that in each laboratory or breeding establishment a single person will be named with overall responsibility for the welfare of the animals.

It is also of primary importance for research workers to explain their objectives to the technicians—which many fail to do. Otherwise an individual who is sympathetically orientated towards the animals under his care, cannot come to terms with the work in hand, namely the ultimate fate of his charges.

2. If animals are bred in the laboratories and kept for experimental purposes they must enjoy the 'five freedoms', recommended for farm animals. In the USA legislation is being formulated which requires exercise for dogs and large animals kept for experimentation—I would endorse this 'sixth freedom', and I also believe that social contact and play are valuable in long-term experiments.

Grants should be tied to this requirement, the head of the department signing the document in person, stating he or she has personally ascertained that this request has been complied with, and will therefore be eligible for a grant for the department.

3. Experiments on living animals should not be regarded as the private concern of the experimenter, but as part of the corporate life of the institution in which they work. Regular meetings should be held under the chairmanship of the head of the department, at which the value of the experiment would be discussed and an attempt made to assess the probable gains to knowledge versus the probable suffering caused. Not only the students and post-doctoral students and scientific staff, but the technicians of every grade should attend these meetings.

The Biology sub-faculty of Oxford University have given us a lead in this direction. A committee has been set up to receive complaints which undergraduates may have concerning the use of live animals in class practicals, and to advise demonstrators on both the legal and ethical aspects of animal care. It has also been suggested that the committee might hold 'open forum' discussions between students and staff on the use of animals in 'practicals' and research projects.

4. Details of how the experiment is to be carried out, how the animal is to be killed or anaesthetized and the post-experimental treatment selected should be discussed frankly, and, if need be, modified, before the work is submitted to

the relevant authority for approval. Again, the technicians should attend such discussions.

5. Scientists would be required to sign a statement with their annual report stating in what way they considered the experiment in question had increased knowledge relevant to human or animal health or wellbeing.

6. The number of experiments on live animals should be reduced. They fell by 4 per cent in 1984, but could be drastically cut. Experiments which patently have no bearing on human or animal welfare should be prohibited. Thus, sufficient cosmetics have already been tested and put on the market to satisfy all but pecuniary gain or fashion, and further experiments in this category on live animals should be phased out quickly or stopped. If new cosmetics are envisaged, only those which can be safely tested on *in vitro* preparations should be considered. We can already buy 'Beauty Without Cruelty' cosmetics in health shops.

7. Students should be taught pharmacology and the practical use of painkilling and anaesthetizing drugs. These should be provided more liberally than at present, both for operations and long-term post-operational pain relief.

8. All examination papers should include questions on the ethics of zoology and physiology, laboratory animals, alternative methods to the use of live animals in research, views on present legislation, and so on. A major lecture should be given on the subject of laboratory animals during the first year of all Natural Science and Medical courses.

9. Editors of scientific journals should categorically refuse to publish papers which describe unethical experiments and techniques.*

The *Journal of Experimental Biology*[64] states:

Experiments on Living Animals. The Editorial Board will not allow the publication of papers describing experimental procedures which may reasonably be presumed to have inflicted unnecessary pain, discomfort,

---

* Examples of papers refused: one in which 120 turtles were drowned; another in which fish were operated on while immobilized with curare.

The International Federation of Scientific Editors' Associations (IFSEA) and its member groups have begun to pay attention to the question of ethics in animal experimentation within their role as gatekeepers of scientific literature. It can be expected that they will promote repetition of the statement of the *Journal of Experimental Biology* (cited above) in all biological journals.

or disturbance of normal health on living animals. Manuscripts will only
be accepted if:

1. It is clear that the advances made in physiological knowledge justified the procedures;
2. Appropriate anaesthetic and surgical procedures were followed;
3. Adequate steps were taken to ensure that animals did not suffer unnecessarily at any stage of the experiment.

Papers on vertebrates will only be accepted if the experiments comply
with the legal requirements of the United Kingdom (see *Handbook for
the Animal Licence Holder*, Institute of Biology; *Notes on the Law
Relating to Experiments on Animals in Great Britain*, Research Defence
Society; UFAW *Handbook on the Care and Management of Laboratory
Animals*) or *Federal Legislation and the National Institutes of Health
Guidelines in the U.S.A. Department of Health, Education and Welfare*,
Publication No. NIH 78-23 (1978).

Animal Behaviour[1] has an ethical committee and on several
occasions recently has refused to publish papers on ethical
grounds. They have also published *Guidelines for the use of
animals in research.*[1]

These are examples which should be followed on a broad
front. There are, in fact, relatively few journals of standing, in
which experimental biologists and physiologists would like to
see their papers published. They present something of a bottle-
neck. Needless to say, such directives are bound to present
lacunae, however carefully worded, and are easily circumvented
by those who wish to do so. Also rules and regulations excite
a spirit of rebellion, so that a schoolboy attitude of 'beating
the inspector' is generated. Nevertheless a clear-cut policy
among the editors of the top journals—with the selection of
well informed referees—would have considerable impact.

10. The attitude of scientists towards Inspectors working for
the Ministry should change. They should encourage criticism
and opt for greater 'clout' for Inspectors and welcome
revelations of irregularities and lack of care that may well
have escaped them.

11. Training in statistics: good experimental design and
appreciation of statistical logic are both excellent means of
reducing the numbers of animals used.

The future

The importance of *in vitro* testing has recently loomed large
on the horizon and one notices with some surprise but great

satisfaction—almost with a tinge of optimism—that substantial prizes are now offered to researchers in this field.

Good films and tapes should take the place of pithed frogs in the classroom, and one hopes that legislation will eventually direct teachers, researchers, and industrial toxicologists away from conscious animals. John Treherne also suggests that, in the long run, computer modelling of pharmacologically active compounds and of their potential target sites will greatly reduce the need of much routine initial screening of pharmaceutical and toxic material.

The different climate of today has, furthermore, turned controversial matters dealing with cruelty to animals, such as the wholesale destruction of habitats, vivisection, and bloodsports, into a politically attractive arena for legislation, not the vote-losing enterprise of the good old days.

THE COUNTRYSIDE

Control

In the 'twenties delicious roast partridge was served for our lunch during the first week of September. My father did not allow shooting game birds for 'sport' but accepted them as a welcome change at the dinner table. The farm manager, who was an excellent shot, flew a kite over certain grass meadows, and the partridges, believing it was a hawk, sat tight. When they eventually rose in panic from almost beneath his feet they proved an easy target. The kite, explained my father, in answer to my rather agitated enquiry, for baby partridges were one of my great loves, ensured that the quarry only flew up within close range and was killed outright, not wounded. It never occurred to me to ask why we had to have partridges for lunch during September, any more than I asked why we were deprived of those delicious thin, game chips at all other times of the year. Somehow both were part of Autumn, like hips and haws, red and yellow leaves and dahlias blackened by frost.

My father recognized the necessity for control in his Nature Reserve,[100] and in his view the balance was disturbed by too many rabbits and too many pheasants which consequently should be reduced in number. Four thousand of the former and about three hundred of the latter were duly shot annually. Snaring was not permitted. Since the process was continuous, it may well have achieved its purpose. At that period (1910-25) there were few arable crops round the reserve, and the wood-pigeons and rooks were left unmolested.

The University Federation for Animal Welfare (UFAW)[10] has publicized the case for humane and reasonable control of pests and 'nuisances'. Their recommendations on shooting, trapping and baiting should be studied and followed. These directions can also be modified to suit the type of control which seeks to strike a balance in Nature Reserves and uncultivated tracts of country. Here Schweitzer's 'agonizing choices' come into play, for the manager must, for instance, attempt to protect trees from the depredation of squirrels and deer, and rare grass-feeding butterfly larvae from too many assiduous pheasants and hornets.

As Charles Elton[29] pointed out, consideration for animals will never take precedence over human survival but the apparent conflict of interests can be modified by the elimination of ignorance—often based on a combination of prejudice and tradition—and the now readily available results of serious research, especially those relating to the most humane methods of killing vertebrates. There is undeniably a wide gap between this information and the people for whom it is intended and who should practise it in the field. The real problem is how to put it across.

Field sports

I loved horses and riding. Both proved exhilarating. I soon discovered you could see more of the countryside, and experience the thrill of getting quite close to the wildlife of the woods and fields from the back of a pony than on two feet. Curiously enough the knowledge I gained in this way gave me a sense of superiority over the folk who walked or drove along roads and well-worn paths. One day a neighbour's daughter, whom I rather admired, suggested I got permission to go 'cubbing' with her. Thereafter I hunted with the local pack of foxhounds twice a week. First and foremost it was an escape from a nagging governess and solitary, insufferably boring lessons; secondly it was a whole day's riding in the company of a group of jolly contemporaries; thirdly it was both interesting and very exciting. I firmly believed what I was told, namely, that only fox-hunting preserved The Fox. Otherwise, like the wolves in England, this lovely animal would have long been exterminated. Now, for each fox hunted and perhaps caught and killed, a score lived happily in the woods. My first uneasy moments occurred when the late John Fryer indicated that one could not unfortunately ask foxes for their views, which, indeed, might be very different from my own. Then one day I was waiting with a group of riders while the hounds were noisily drawing a small cover alongside us. Suddenly a slim red fox emerged from the bushes, ran for a few yards into the field, stopped to urinate and then fled on towards a distant hedgerow. It looked very small and frightened. One of the women riders laughed loudly. *'Do* you see *that?'* she cried. 'It's actually sitting down!'

I suddenly realized, with a prickly feeling beneath my scalp, that this pastime was extremely cruel. I gave up hunting.

The climate is changing rapidly and there can be little doubt that even if the private members' bills shortly to be considered by the House of Commons[19, 90] are defeated, the next Labour Government will bring in legislation to abolish hunting with dogs. There is of course a perfectly adequate substitute in the form of hunting a drag. This already takes place in quite large areas of Canada[76] where foxes are afflicted with rabies and therefore cannot be handled. All the traditional aspects of the sport are preserved; the dressing up in coloured coats; the horses; the hounds; the cameraderie; fun for the children: the excitement of steeplechasing; and, of course, the vested interests in all the varied aspects of the game. The only element lacking is the uncertainty resulting from the pursuit of a live animal. There are a few people who have developed a great interest and not a little skill in the craft of hunting with hounds and who consequently cling to a live quarry. But the great majority of followers know nothing about it at all. They are aware that there are days when there is a 'good' scent and a 'bad' scent and they have read of a 'breast-high' scent, but if hounds checked and the huntsman enquired of the field if he should cast down wind or up wind he would be met with blank stares of incomprehension.

If you are conditioned in your teens to follow a drag instead of a fox you will enjoy the performance just as keenly. You will not regret the change any more than the young skier of today hankers after the telemark. (What is a telemark?) The huntsman dressed in red with a white, blue, or black collar, as the case may be, can still exhibit his hounds at Peterborough show and return clutching a silver pot to his chest. Your hunter class at Olympia will be equally magnificent and the rosettes just as desirable. Fortunately the switch from fox to drag involves no agonizing choices. In fact how can a sane man or woman hesitate to make this change?

Hunter trials and show jumping today—due in part to the media—have become immensely popular and there is little doubt that hunting a drag, a rather different form of old fashioned steeplechasing, would follow suit. In their review of the economic significance of country sports the Standing Conference[18] estimated that 240 000 people hunted with hounds (in 1982), 3 000 people were employed by the organizers of the sport, and a total of £102 million was spent each year by both organizers and participants. I would guess that these figures might increase substantially if drag was substituted for the fox and a wider and more varied section of the riding community would participate.

Shooting is a different matter, for it is probably the most reliable and humane method of culling wild animals. If, in the case of pheasants, rabbits, hares, and deer, it can at the same time be carried out as a pleasurable sport which gives enjoyment to many people, there is no reason to legislate against it—always providing the animals concerned are killed outright. In order to reduce the number of wounded victims (a few are inevitable) gun licences should be issued only to those sportsmen who have passed a proficiency test. This is the law in West Germany, Holland, Denmark, France, and in various other European countries. The standards required in Sweden are very tough. No one should be allowed to carry a gun, any more than anyone can drive a car, without first passing a test. It is a sobering thought that in 1982 there were twenty-two deaths in the UK due to accidents with shotguns.[88] Today owners of shoots invariably count the number of birds shot. It would be better to count the number of birds wounded, and discreetly cull their guns accordingly.

Shooting like hunting is a social amusement* but unfortunately owners of shoots, both for personal kudos and pecuniary gain, consider it necessary to provide their guests with a large number of targets. It has therefore become fashionable to rear pheasants in pens, release them in the area

* Many people who shoot today are visitors to, rather than residents in the country. They have very little knowledge of wildlife or the countryside, and quite often cannot distinguish between a field of barley and one of wheat, or tell a red-legged partridge from a common partridge. They also have a scanty knowledge of firearms and game conservation.

and then drive these tame birds before the guns to be blown to bits or maimed. It is hardly necessary to comment on this lamentable practice, which is a sad relic from the past, reaching its zenith in Edwardian times[101] when wealthy land-owners vied with each other for personal aggrandizement by producing the most impressive bags. Today farmers and land-owners can add substantially to their incomes by letting their land to shooting syndicates, and many consider it essential, if they are to keep their customers, to rear and release a lot of tame birds to add to the fun.

There is one great benefit we owe to sportsmen and that is the preservation of small covers and woodlands, for they would have been cut down and ploughed up years ago but for the sake of the game they shelter. Recent research by the Game Conservancy[42] has shown us how we can further the cause of field sport by a wider concept and practice of con-servation.

Deer are one of the most unexpected success stories of the last decades. Who would have dreamed, forty years ago, that so many woodlands in the UK would harbour deer by 1985?[89] It is a surprise bonus for which I believe we have to thank the Forestry Commission. Fallow deer, Roe Deer, Sika and Muntjak—they are all graceful, nervous, and charming creatures, and many people shrink at the thought of shooting or wounding them. At present this seems to involve less cruelty and stress than netting and sending them—terrified—by motor transport to the slaughterhouse.[35] Eventually one hopes improved narcotic baiting will solve the problem of culling deer—wild or farmed—humanely. Stalkers, here as elsewhere, should be required by legislation to use telescopic sights.

There is undoubtedly today an increased awareness among field sportsmen that the wellbeing of wildlife hinges on con-serving and providing the right habitat, and farmers are gradually coming round to the same opinion; a very success-ful one near Cambridge has now put back many of the hedges he grubbed up twenty years ago and, I notice, has introduced a fair proportion of wild roses among his bushes.

Fishing is the most popular field sport in Britain. Accord-ing to the Standing Conference on Countryside Sports[18]

there were over 3 780 000 participants in the game in the UK.
It is also of greater economic significance than any other field
sport and more people are directly employed through fishing
than in all the others combined. There can be no argument
about whether or not fishing is unkind. It is. For pleasure, a
harmless and inoffensive animal is hooked in the mouth with
a metal barb ... Tugging against it, with its full weight behind the pull must be excruciatingly painful, like an endlessly
prolonged tooth extraction.* If fish could scream aloud,
the Exchequer might lose the revenue from, say, a million
licences. It always seems strange to me that fly fisherwomen
especially glory in the long battle to land their salmon, and
with shining eyes and flushed cheeks describe the moment of
triumph. I once asked a beautiful girl, highly skilled with rod
and line—who incidentally spent much of her life nursing sick
and dying people in refugee camps—if she had any sympathy
for this handsome animal, which had done her no disservice
and lived quietly out of sight, doing its thing, in a separate
world. She said no, in her view it was a natural fate for
animals to be hunted. It was part of Nature. I persisted.
'Would you flinch if, instead of simply thrashing about in
the water, the salmon could shriek and beg for mercy, would
you then go on playing it for 30 minutes?' She said yes, she
expected she would, although it was a hypothetical question,
because it was part of the nature of things.

Fishing gives a lot of people a lot of pleasure and nowa-
days many anglers put their fish back in the river ... Furthermore this sport brings numbers of individuals into contact
with Nature, who otherwise would never know the first thing
about wildlife and the countryside. It is in fact highly bene-
ficial—psychologically—for the fishermen, and, perhaps, the
rivers and their plant life get a little additional consideration
in consequence. Several million animals are sacrificed annually
in the laboratory for the sake of our physical health and
beauty. Leaving aside all the economic facets of the sport, is
there something to be said for sacrificing—painfully—a few

* The structure of the fish's brain is different from that of mammals. It could
be argued that, when lacking cerebral hemispheres, they do not consciously experience pain, however violently they may react to stimulation.

million fish every year for about 40 million hours of our pleasure and contentment? Perhaps there is.

Suggestions

1. Proficiency certificates must be produced before a gun licence or a licence for a rifle is issued to any individual.*

2. Telescopic sights should be compulsory for shooting deer.

3. Birds should not be reared in captivity and released and shot merely to increase the bag.

4. Air-guns and air-weapons. Between the ages of 15–18, a licence must be obtained and the guns used only for target shooting. (As in Sweden.)

5. Fox-hunting should be switched to drag–hunting. In any case legislation to abolish fox-hunting is anticipated. Possibly hunting a drag once a week now would prepare the way for a smooth changeover and also ensure that the existing traditions of individual packs could be maintained.

6. Many farmers are already keeping certain headlands and verges unsprayed especially with game preservation in view. They should be compensated for the conservation of refuges and unsprayed hedges (other than those scheduled in the *Wildlife and Countryside Act* of 1981).[118] In Germany there is a movement to compensate farmers also for strips of unsprayed arable crops.

7. Gin traps are now illegal in the UK. But a greater effort should be made to find more humane traps to replace snares which are remarkably cheap and efficient but cause the trapped animals hours of acute stress. Foxes caught in snares injure themselves severely. Furthermore although the *Countryside Act* (1981) requires snares to be visited once daily this is frequently neglected.

8. A much greater effort should be made to find painless narcotic baits suitable for controlling deer, rabbits, moles, and mink. At present the most effective way of killing moles is with strychnine-doctored worms. Providing a permit is obtained to kill moles in this manner, it is a simple matter to

* I will not enter into the discussion of the relative merits of voluntary or mandatory Testing Schemes but refer the reader to the British Association for Shooting and Conservation Research Officer at Marford Mill, Rossett, Clwyd.

buy strychnine from the chemist—and it is well known that this dangerous poison is frequently used for baiting other animals above ground.*

A narcotic bait is available for catching deer but it is unselective and one is apt to catch the wrong age-group and wrong sex, even if the various species can be segregated. Further research is required.

9. Lead weights of a specific size used by anglers will shortly become illegal. The loss of swans due to lead poisoning after ingesting these weights is a reminder that one should exercise care in the pursuit of all field sports. Fishermen have drawn attention to the amount of lead sprayed into the rivers by duck shooters and one wonders if continuous clay-pigeon shooting in one area is a potential danger to local birds.

* In the Oxford area I myself lost a dog which picked up liver injected with strychnine, put down to kill foxes. The Royal Society for the Protection of Birds (RSPB) in 1981 reported 42 dogs which died of poisoning. (See also Cadbury, 1980)[12]

THE HOME

As a child I owned a tough fox terrier called Nelly, who slept under my bed. Like so many of her breed she found moving objects irresistible—chasing and killing my grandfather's pinioned ornamental pheasants, as well as streaking after motor vehicles. My mother, who knew how deeply I loved Nelly, concealed her depredations from my grandfather, but one fine day the little dog was killed chasing a motor-cycle down Tring High Street. The nursemaid bustled me along so that I never saw Nelly lying in the road but I still recall my deeply shocked disbelief. Surely Nelly's twinkling paws could never stop moving? 'Shall I meet Nelly again in Heaven?' I asked the nursemaid, in an agonized whisper. 'No', replied the girl authoritatively. 'Dogs are animals—they don't go to Heaven.'

It never occurred to me to ask her how she knew. I accepted what grown-ups said as if they were in direct communication with the Almighty, but from that moment onwards I became secretly highly critical of God. If dogs were not admitted, I had little use for Heaven either. Curiously enough, although I chattered freely and incessantly with my parents about the events of the day, I never discussed these feelings, which seemed to belong to something apart.

A replacement, 'Susie', was duly found for poor Nelly. Looking back, I fancy my dogs were considerably more important to me than my siblings. I never felt an urge to photograph my brother or sisters and certainly I never dreamed of writing their tedious lifestories, whereas I planned to immortalize Susie with an illustrated biography and spent all my pocket money on films for that purpose. Susie was uncooperative. (I have never yet owned a dog which liked being photographed. At the sight of the camera one and all would slink away, and if obedient to a command to sit still, lashed back their ears and assumed an expression of acute misery.)

Nor did I worry much when my sisters were punished, bumped their heads, or went down with influenza, but I minded acutely if my dogs were scolded or sick. Furthermore I never planned to give my brother or sisters their favourite chocolates or sweets, nor a 'good time', whereas I regularly sneaked titbits for Susie and, to please her, took her rabbiting every afternoon. Susie was a desperately keen but inept hunter, but one day she actually appeared carrying a moribund baby rabbit. It was still warm, but, at this age, I felt no compassion, only immense satisfaction on her behalf. I lavished praise upon her: 'Good Susie, clever, *clever* Susie!' She looked smug. At last I got a snapshot—a bit out of focus due to the excitement of the unbelievable happening. For me camaraderie and larks and rivalry and demon patience were shared enthusiastically with the siblings; but solicitude, affection, and caring were reserved for Susie.

As far as I was concerned the long line of dogs which followed Susie down to the present day each taught me something. 'Anyone who has kept a horse or a dog' wrote Alister Hardy,[50] 'and got really fond of them can't doubt that they are conscious beings like ourselves.'

In the western world we are rather uncaring for the old members of the community—unlike the Chinese—but we have one saving grace which makes up for our multiple sins of omission: we have selectively bred dogs which are fond of us, young and old people alike.

Looking back I realize that a dog or a cat in the home is the most powerful tool there is for teaching children how to behave, how to care, and the meaning of goodwill. Unfortunately few even affluent parents seize this opportunity, nor do they give serious thought to the requirements of their pets. It is customary to see children dragging a dog along, mercilessly, by a collar and lead, without eliciting a word of reproof or explanation from their adult companions.

That individuals care about the welfare of animals is illustrated by the fact that the Royal Society for the Prevention of Cruelty to Animals (RSPCA, which incidentally is a voluntary organization relying entirely on private subscriptions) received over a million calls 'for help' in 1984.[102, 105] The reverse side of this coin is the depressing fact that this figure included 250 000 more cases than during the previous year. There are only 220 uniformed RSPCA inspectors serving throughout the UK—more are needed.

A cursory glance at the convictions obtained by the RSPCA last year shows that neglect and abandonment are the chief problems where dogs and cats are concerned.[105] This is often due to owners not realizing, when they acquire a puppy or a kitten, what a tie the animal becomes. What is to be done if the family wants a holiday for a week or more, for the cost of 'boarding' animals is prohibitive. Again, how can they meet the rising cost of animal food? How costly would it be to dispose of the dog? What would a vet charge? One way of assisting with the problem of abandonment is to issue a brief leaflet with the dog licence stating the cost of keeping a dog, its requirements, and, if the necessity arises, how to get rid of it without causing suffering, and at the lowest possible cost.

Perhaps it is a little far-fetched to consider fur coats under the heading of animals in the home but this is relevant to the upbringing of children. I need hardly say that in my personal view the fur trade should be phased out, and successful actresses should find a better way of advertising their Oscars. In this part of home life we have one singularly cheering precedent. Before World War I, two or three hundred million tropical birds were killed annually to supply the millinery trade.[53] Not only is the importing of foreign bird feathers now illegal, but no women would contemplate appearing in a hat decorated with birds of paradise plumes. Doubtless in time—one hopes soon—fur coats will suffer the same fate as feather hats, especially since synthetic substitutes are now available. It will be a good moment when a parent can say to a child, 'Believe it or not people used to wear fur coats—yes, baby seal coats—and put humming bird feathers in their hats . . .'

The following guidelines are suggested for improving the lot of animals kept in the home:

1. Every school should teach pet-care and respect for animal and plant life to their pupils both to very young classes and to older children. Parents should be encouraged to join such classes. (The Education Department of the RSPCA has published an excellent booklet on *Animals in Schools*.)[104]

2. Dog licences should be issued with a leaflet giving a brief outline of the animal's requirements, a vet's address and telephone number, advice on how to have a dog or cat neutered, and how to get rid of an unwanted animal without causing suffering and with minimal expense.*

3. Personnel in pet shops should be trained in proper pet care and no licence to sell live animals should be issued without proof that the applicant's staff has the necessary expertise.

4. The sale of sadistic videotapes and films showing mutilation, violence and terrifying cruelty to animals should be banned.

Further considerations

The RSPCA, who were called upon to destroy 141 000 dogs and cats in the UK in 1984,[105] are strongly in favour of neutering pet bitches and female cats, for the sheer weight of offspring from unwanted breeding results in numerous cases of abandonment. They also advocate an increased cost for licences and this is sound policy providing that pensioners are exempted. In addition, the cost of the licence would be reduced for neuterered animals; these dogs are also usually less aggressive than entire animals but it must be realized that the cost of spaying a bitch is £40. Furthermore the increase in the dog licence should be used to combat animal neglect and not be diverted by the Treasury for other purposes.

We are concerned with two different sets of problems for pets in rural districts or cities. Many people who would like to own a dog consider it cruel to keep them in a town, where exercising them is difficult and they are of necessity confined in a small space while their owners are at work. Straying dogs cause car accidents in heavy traffic and also foul the streets. In France they are banned from many open spaces, for they render them unhealthy as children's playgrounds. Some cities in the USA insist that dog-owners carry a receptacle in which they collect their dog's faeces, but this does not control the activities of animals which run free in the streets

---

* There is a good case for allowing vets to receive a subsidy for this service, thus making it a free service for a pet owner.

and gardens, with or without their owners. There is no doubt that in cities there is an over-population of dogs and a good case could be made out for banning the sale of live dogs and cats in pet shops. An appealing puppy or kitten in the window often results in a purchase from the heart rather than the head, resulting in an 'animal welfare problem'. There is no doubt that elderly people who live in flats would be less worried by a budgerigar than a pet dog. Many such dog owners are deeply concerned about the future of their pet, should they themselves die. They could consider a bird rather than a dog if they are acquiring a companion animal in old age. This problem is less acute in rural districts where a good home for a dog is relatively easy to find, but in towns it will be difficult to provide a satisfactory solution. Under the proposed legislation at least old folk will be spared the anxiety that their dog may be rounded up and taken away for laboratory experiments,[2] for under the new Act this will become illegal.

CONCLUSIONS

One can sense natural selection at work in the protracted evolution in one's own life, from the innocent child to the callous youth—moulded by the environment and the 'acceptancy' period of one's early teens—then on to the so-called 'reasonable' adult, and finally to the more philosophical, if rheumaticky, sentient old man or woman. Vince Dethier[28] marvels at the fact that the atrocities we perpetrate against animals have all been practised in the immediate past or in the present, on our fellow men and women. 'The behaviour of men to the lower animals' remarked Herbert Spencer,[111] 'and their behaviour to each other, bear a constant relationship.' Perhaps the most important change in our time is that, thanks to television and radio, we know more about what goes on. We may run the risk of becoming inured against the plethora of horrors shown to us, from bombs, and massacres, earthquakes and famine, to chickens squeezed into concentration camp-like cages. But at least we can no longer plead ignorance.

At this point it would be easy to wander off into a philosophical or theological argument concerning compassion and the better treatment of animals. Jon Wynne-Tyson[120] has just published a dictionary of humane thought and sums up his conclusions in a quotation from Alfred Schweitzer who says, 'Until he extends the circle of his compassion to all living things man will not himself find peace.' But it is the immediate and practical future that concerns me. Have we the slightest cause for optimism? Perhaps just a flicker.

As far as laboratory animals are concerned it is the change in our own moral evolution that looks most promising. The callous youth has, to quite a considerable degree, transformed into the questioning and dissatisfied student. Dissent and criticism usually come from the young and are directed against the elderly—entrenched in their conventional LD 50s, convivial bloodsports, and their pithed frogs. Clive Hollands[58] believes we are entering a fresh era in the UK, with the enactment of the new legislation and that there is 'a growing trust between those involved in both sides of the issue'. I am less optimistic but I agree emphatically with Hollands that hope springs from the fact that there is a change in the way those involved in research (especially the young) think of animals.

Secondly, the more enlightened Swedes—a precursory nation—have launched a modest £20 million[84] five-year agricultural plan to eradicate factory farming. They intend to pay greater attention to the wellbeing of the animals raised for slaughter and stimulate research into alternative agricultural methods. The Swedes have a high standard of living—something which lightens the burden on animals—and their country is not overpopulated. In a crowded rat cage or a crowded city the more vicious and aggressive side of our natures are stimulated. Where the students and the Swedes lead, in time, I fancy, we will follow. We need that grain of comfort.

APPENDIX

REPORT ON THE WELFARE OF LIVESTOCK (RED MEAT)
ANIMALS AT THE TIME OF SLAUGHTER:
SUMMARY OF RECOMMENDATIONS*

Recommendations for legislation

1. At every slaughterhouse, the local authority to designate an official with formal responsibility for supervising compliance with welfare requirements. The official to be the Official Veterinary Surgeon where present, and an Environmental Health Officer (Veterinary Meat Inspector in Scotland) in other premises (paras. 16 and 17).

2. The designated official to be allowed time to carry out these duties and to be required to report breaches of welfare regulations, etc. to the Chief Environr..ental Health Officer (para. 17).

3. Officers of the State Veterinary Service should be required to visit all licensed slaughterhouses to check on compliance with welfare requirements on a regular basis and to report their findings to the Chief Environmental Health Officer (para. 18).

4. Annual licensing to be a requirement for all Scottish slaughterhouses (para. 26).

5. When considering applications for new slaughterhouse licences and for licence renewals, local authorities should be required to take account of advice from the State Veterinary Service (para. 26).

6. Purpose-built unloading bays must be provided when new slaughterhouse premises are being constructed (para. 31).

7. Animals held in lairages must have sufficient space to stand up, lie down and turn around (para. 45).

8. Regulation 7 of the *Slaughter of Animals (Prevention of Cruelty) Regulations 1958*, relating to frequency of feeding animals held in lairages, should be simplified and account also taken of the needs of individual species, the effects of travelling time, etc. (paras. 51 and 52. See also Recommendations 89 and 112).

9. The regulation requiring restraint of horned cattle when penned together should be reviewed (para. 54).

10. Existing legislation to be amended to permit the use of 'Judas sheep' in slaughterhouses (para. 65).

11. A general provision, on the lines of Section 4(2)(a) of the Transit of Animals (Road and Rail) Order 1975, for prohibiting excessive use of goads, etc., should be introduced for handling animals in the slaughterhouse (para. 66).

* A report prepared by the Farm Animal Welfare Council. © Crown Copyright 1984.

12. In the approach races and stunning areas the use of sticks or plastic piping to strike animals should be prohibited and the use of electric goads should be permitted only to the hindquarters of animals refusing to move forward (para. 66).

13. Legislation should clearly distinguish between the two stages of slaughter, i.e. stunning and sticking (para. 80).

14. The existing prohibition on slaughter of animals within the sight of others to be amended to relate to sticking only. Stunning within the sight of others to be allowed but only subject to specified safeguards. Scottish legislation to be brought into line with this (paras. 80 and 83).

15. A responsible member of the slaughterhouse staff to carry out checks, at least daily, that animals are being effectively stunned (para. 88).

16. Slaughter techniques which both stun and kill should be provided for within legislation (para. 93).

17. Animals should not be placed in a stunning box until the way is clear for them to be stunned, slaughtered and bled (para. 106).

18. Cattle stunning boxes be required to contain a head restraining device (para. 107).

19. Where a slaughterman is stunning and sticking a batch of animals singlehanded, both operations must be completed consecutively for each animal (para. 120).

20. The shackling of animals should be prohibited while the animal remains on its feet (para. 121).

21. Legislation should specifically ban the hanging of animals before stunning (para. 121).

22. Electric tongs must not be used other than for stunning an animal (para. 128).

23. Manual electrical stunning systems must incorporate a warning light or buzzer to indicate necessary period of application (para. 131).

24. Electrical stunning systems must incorporate a fail-safe device to prevent operating with a lower than required current (para. 131).

25. Electrical stunning equipment should be subject to regular checks (para. 132).

26. Operators of electrical stunning systems should be required to abide by manufacturers' guidelines on the correct voltage and current, correct time of application and correct positioning of electrodes (paras. 133 and 137).

27. Stunning of cattle in the poll position should be banned (para. 147).

28. Operators of captive bolt pistols should be required to abide by manufacturers' instructions on the correct positioning of the pistol, weight of charge used and sharpness of the bolt (para. 154).

29. All stunning equipment should be subject to monthly checks by the slaughterhouse licensing authority (para. 161).

30. Manufacturers of all stunning equipment should be required to meet criteria set as a matter of urgency in legislation, and be required to specify in the operating instructions the correct positioning and, where

applicable, correct stunning times and currents, etc. necessary for effective operation of the equipment concerned (para. 162).

31. A reserve stunning instrument of the captive bolt type must be readily available for use in the event of a breakdown of the main stunning system (para. 163).

32. Licensing authorities must ensure that correct sticking procedures have been understood and adopted by slaughtermen to whom licences are issued (para. 168).

33. The use of electrical stimulation treatment should be permitted only on animals which have been both stunned and stuck (para. 172).

34. Use of tenderizing by injection of the enzyme papain should be banned, and such a ban should cover any process which involves the forcible administration of a preparation or drug within 24 hours of slaughter for other than therapeutic reasons (para. 182).

35. All emergency slaughter animals to be put down on the farm and not transported for slaughter (para. 189).

36. All casualty slaughter animals over the age of two months dispatched live for slaughter must be accompanied by a veterinary certificate which includes a declaration that the animal is fit to travel and specifies the slaughterhouse to which it is to be consigned (para. 190).

37. The designated official responsible for welfare should check that casualty slaughter requirements are being properly met and report any breaches to the enforcement authority (para. 190).

38. All slaughterhouses should be required to display the telephone number of a contact for casualty slaughter outside normal working hours (para. 191).

39. All slaughterhouses should have facilities for slaughtering animals on the transporters and be required to use them in appropriate circumstances (para. 192).

40. Slaughterhouses should be required to have trolleys for the movement of sick and injured smaller species (para. 192).

41. The slaughter of casualty animals which are in pain or suffering must not be delayed (para. 193—see also Recommendation 62).

42. The designated official responsible for welfare in the slaughterhouse should be required to advise the local Divisional Veterinary Officer where there is reason to believe that proper consideration is not being given to welfare on the farm of origin (para. 194).

43. Full licences should not be issued to slaughtermen with no previous experience and provisional licences should be introduced to allow a trainee to operate only under supervision for a prescribed period (para. 199).

44. Full licences should be in a form prescribed by legislation, should specify the stunning and slaughter methods and species concerned and should certify that new licences have undergone a period of supervized training (para. 199).

45. Before issuing a full licence, a suitably qualified or experienced local authority official should be required to observe the slaughterman

operating the stunning and slaughter equipment concerned on all species for which his licence is required (para. 199).

46. Specific responsibility for animal welfare should be allocated to a nominated member of the slaughterhouse staff (para. 204).

47. Formalized training should be given to slaughtermen, particularly in relation to the needs of the animals and the operation of stunning and slaughter equipment (para. 205).

48. Rabbits at slaughter should be given the full protection of legislation enjoyed by other species (para. 214).

49. Such legislation should accommodate stunning or instantaneous killing by the 'sharp blow' method (para. 214).

50. In relation to lairing, feeding and watering, account should be taken of the recommendations contained in the *Welfare Code for Rabbits* (para. 214).

51. Animals slaughtered on the farm should be humanely handled and killed instantaneously (para. 218).

Recommendations for better enforcement

52. Local authorities to make more use of their enforcement powers (para. 19).

53. Agriculture Departments to take enforcement action if local authorities do not use their powers (para. 19).

54. Local authorities to be reminded of their enforcement responsibilities under the Transit of Animals (Road and Rail) Order 1975, particularly relating to lorry unloading facilities, non-slip surfaces, protection of animals awaiting unloading, and unloading without causing injury or unnecessary suffering (paras. 30, 32–34).

55. More account to be taken of the provisions of Regulation 11 of the *Slaughterhouses (Hygiene) Regulations 1977* relating to the state of repair of non-slip floors and surfaces (para. 31).

56. There should be better enforcement of the provisions in the *Slaughter of Animals (Prevention of Cruelty) Regulations 1958* relating to lairage accommodation and use (para. 40).

57. Drinking facilities in lairages should be subject to more regular checks (para. 50).

58. There is a need to ensure that food and feeding facilities provided in lairages are suitable (para. 53).

59. Animals laired away from the curtilage of the slaughterhouse should benefit from the surveillance provisions in the relevant legislation (para. 55).

60. There should be better enforcement of Section 36(1) of the *Slaughterhouses Act 1974* and Regulation 16 of the *Slaughter of Animals (Prevention of Cruelty) Regulations 1958* relating to stunning (para. 124).

61. There should be better enforcement of the provisions of the *Agriculture (Miscellaneous Provisions) Act 1968* and the *Transit of Animals (Road and Rail) Order 1975* in relation to handling and transportation of casualty animals (para. 187).

62. Regulation 18 of the *Slaughter of Animals (Prevention of Cruelty) Regulations 1958*, requiring slaughter of animals in pain without delay, should be properly enforced (para. 193).

Recommendations for proposed Code of Practice

63. Animals to be handled in a calm, unhurried manner (paras. 28 and 56).

64. More use should be made of hydraulic tail-lifts or adjustable unloading bays to accommodate unloading from multi-tier lorries (para. 30).

65. The use of guide boards for pigs is recommended (para. 34).

66. An experienced stockman should be responsible for handling livestock in the unloading and lairage areas (para. 35).

67. Slatted and mesh floors must be properly cleansed and maintained to avoid injury to the animals (para. 42).

68. There should be provision for adequate exchange of air facilities (paras. 47 and 48).

69. Lighting must be sufficient to allow for proper inspection of animals (para. 49).

70. Drinking facilities in lairages must be accessible for the species housed (para. 50).

71. Animals should not be held for lengthy periods in the approach races to the stunning areas (para. 57).

72. Metal gates, doors, and fittings to be baffled against noise (paras. 58 and 109).

73. Animals must be securely penned in the lairage and no opportunities given for escape from the approach races (para. 62).

74. Facility to be provided for obtaining access to base of stunning box (para. 105).

75. The design of cattle stunning boxes should allow for animals to be evacuated and returned to the lairage (para. 106).

76. Moveable parts of cattle stunning boxes to be fitted with noise absorbent baffles (para. 109).

77. Cattle boxes to be designed to accommodate both large and small cattle with facility for stunning at different levels (para. 112).

78. Incorporation of a form of restraint in stunning pens for smaller species is favoured (para. 117).

79. Once stunned, animals should be shackled, hung and bled with a minimum of delay (para. 120).

80. Automatic restraining systems should contain facilities for evacuation of the animal (para. 122).

81. Diagrammatic advice on correct positioning of stunning equipment for individual species to be provided (para. 147).

82. Guidelines to be included on correct sticking procedures (para. 168).

83. Contacts for casualty slaughter should be shown in local telephone directories (para. 191).

84. Casualty slaughtering facilities should be within easy access of unloading areas (para. 193).

85. Slaughterhouse managements should be involved and take an interest in the welfare of stock handled in their premises and in the training and scrutiny of their staff (para. 204).

86. Information should be given to slaughterhouse staff in the course of their training, relating both to the needs of the animals and the operation and effect of the equipment they are using (para. 205 — see also Recommendation 47).

87. With electrical stunning of rabbits progress to sticking must not follow too rapidly (para. 211).

Recommendations for research

88. High priority to be given to allocating funds for research work (para. 21).

89. Effects of provision or deprivation of food prior to slaughter (para. 51).

90. To establish (a) signs which indicate that an animal is completely insensible and (b) to what extent reflex actions and movement post-stunning and sticking indicate awareness of pain (para. 89).

91. The use of alternative materials to reduce noise levels (para. 109).

92. Whether animals' attention is attracted to a light source (para. 110).

93. Effectiveness of low-voltage stunning in rendering animals instantaneously insensible to pain (para. 135).

94. Effects of head to back stunning (para. 139).

95. Use of high frequency electrical stunning systems (para. 143).

96. Effect on animals, particularly during the early stages of application, of CO_2 stunning (para. 160).

Other recommendations

Design and construction

97. Unloading bays (para. 31).

98. Solid wall pens in lairages, particularly for pigs (para. 46).

99. Long narrow pens (para. 46).

100. Mobile end walls or gates to move animals down through pens (para. 46).

101. Provision of air conditioning (para. 47).

102. Use of water sprinklers (paras. 48 and 63).

103. Construction of approach races (para. 57).

104. Gradients of approach races (para. 59).

105. Lighting in approach races (para. 61).

106. Working environment (para. 103).

107. Design features for cattle stunning boxes (paras. 105 and 107 to 112).

108. Design features for stunning pens for smaller species (paras. 117 to 119).

109. Use of automatic restrainers (paras. 122 and 137).

110. Use of automatic stunning systems (para. 141).

General

111. More care needs to be taken in the designing of slaughterhouses (para. 23).

112. Consideration to be given to the introduction of a table, prescribing time limits within which animals must be fed in lairages (para. 52—see also Recommendation 8).

113. Advisory code to be considered for use as a plain man's guide to use of electrical stunning systems (para. 144).

114. Consideration to be given to requiring local authorities to arrange for a slaughterhouse to provide a seven-day casualty slaughter service (para. 191).

115. Consideration be given to the development of an apprenticeship/day-release training scheme for slaughtermen (para. 206).

116. Consideration to be given to setting guidelines on maximum throughput rates at the point of slaughter and stunning (para. 207).

117. Relevant recommendations contained in the report to be related to knackers' yards (para. 217).

REFERENCES

1. Animal Behaviour (1981) Guidelines for the use of animals in research. *Animal Behaviour* **29**, 1-2.
2. Animals (Scientific Procedures) Bill (1985) Bill 123. Parliamentary Session 1985-6. And: *Hansard*, House of Lords, 3rd February, 1986. **470**, No. 37, Col. 895. HMSO, London.
3. Balls, M. (1984) Review of man and mouse: animals in medical research. *Alternatives to Laboratory Animals* **12**, 47.
4. —— (1985) Guilt by association: the Glasgow-Pennsylvania connection. *Frame News* **7**, 1-2.
5. Basso, E.B. (1973) *The Kalapalo Indians of Central Brazil*. Holt, Rinehart & Winston, New York.
6. Baxter, M. (1984) *Animal welfare*. North of Scotland College of Agriculture Digest **8**, 3-6.
7. Black, M. (1968) *The labyrinth of language*. Praeger, New York.
8. Bonner, John Tyler (1980) *The evolution of culture in animals*. Princeton University Press, Princeton.
9. Brambell, R.W. (Chairman) (1965) *Report of the Technical Committee to enquire into the welfare of animals kept under intensive livestock husbandry systems*. Command Paper 2836, HMSO, London.
10. Britt, D.P. (ed.) (1985) *Humane control of land mammals and birds*. (Proceedings of a Symposium held at the University of Surrey, Guildford 17-19 September, 1984.) Universities Federation for Animal Welfare, Potters Bar.
11. Budiansky, S. (1984) Laboratory animals: Berkeley fined for violations. *Nature* **310**, 356.
12. Cadbury, J.C. (1980) *Silent Death. The destruction of birds through the deliberate misuse of poisons in Britain*. Royal Society for the Protection of Birds, Bedfordshire.
13. Campbell, J. (1984) *Historical Atlas of World Mythology. Vol. I. The way of the animal powers*. Times Books, London.
14. Caro, J. (1564) *Shulhkan Arukh* (The Laid Table). First published in Italy.
15. Carson, G. (1972) *Men, Beasts and God. A history of cruelty and kindness to animals*. Scribner's, New York.
16. Chomsky, N. (1966) *Cartesian linguistics*. Harper & Row, New York.
17. Clark, K. (1977) *Animals and Men*. Thames & Hudson, London.
18. Countryside Sports, Standing Committee on (1983). *Countryside Sports: Their Economic Significance*. Foreword by Lord Porchester. Survey by Cobham Resource Consultants. Standing Committee on Countryside Sports, c/o College of Estate Management, Reading University, Reading.

19. Cruelty to Animals (Amendment) Bill (1985) 15th January. HMSO, London.
20. Darwin, C. (1871) Letter to Ray Lankester, March 22nd 1871. (Quoted in F. Darwin, see Ref. 23 below.)
21. — (1881) Letter to the Times, 22nd April 1881. (Quoted in F. Darwin, see Ref. 23 below.)
22. — (1881) Letter to Frithiof Holmgren, April 14th 1881. (Quoted in F. Darwin, see Ref. 23 below.)
23. Darwin, F. (ed.) (1892) *Charles Darwin: his life told in an autobiographical chapter, and in a selected series of his published letters.* John Murray, London.
24. David, P. (1984) N.I.H. to lay down the law. *Nature*, 308, 680.
25. Dawkins, M.S. (1980) *Animal suffering. The Science of animal welfare.* Chapman & Hall, London.
26. Dawkins, R. (1976) *The Selfish Gene.* Oxford University Press, Oxford.
27. Descartes, R. (1978) *Descartes.* Harvester Press, Sussex.
28. Dethier, V. (1985) *In litt.*
29. Elton, C.S. (1958) *The ecology of invasions by animals and plants.* Methuen, London.
30. Encyclopaedia Judaica (1978) Keter Publishing House, Jerusalem.
31. Everton, A.R. (1985) *The protection of farm livestock: avoidance of 'unnecessary suffering' or the positive promotion of welfare?* MS April 1985.
32. Farm Animal Welfare Council (1982) *Report on the welfare of poultry at the time of slaughter.* HMSO, London.
33. — (1984) *Report on the welfare of livestock (red meat animals) at the time of slaughter.* Ref. book. 248, HMSO, London.
34. — (1985) *Report on the welfare of livestock when slaughtered by religious methods.* Ref. book 262, HMSO, London.
35. — (1985) *Report on the welfare of farmed deer.* Booklet 2498, HMSO, London.
36. Fisher, J. and Hinde, R.A. (1949) The opening of milk bottles by birds. *British Birds* 42, 347-57.
37. Fisher, M.P. (1983) Of pigs and dogs. Pets as produce in three societies. In *New perspectives on our lives with companion animals.* (eds. A.H. Katcher and A.M. Beck) pp. 132-7. University of Pennsylvania Press, Philadelphia.
38. Frame News (1984) Summary of statistics of experiments on living animals in Great Britain in 1983. *Frame News*, 3, 2.
39. — (1985) Newsletter of the Fund for the Replacement of Animals in Medical Experiments. *Frame News*, 7, 3.
40. Freud, S. (1938) *Totem and taboo.* Penguin Books, London.
41. Gallup Poll (1985) *Vital statistics — meat eating.* Gallup Poll commissioned by the Realeat Company. 15th May 1985.
42. Game Conservancy (1985) *Annual review.* Spring, 16, 109. (See also Reports for earlier years.)
43. Graur, D. (1985) Down with Animal Lib. *Nature,* 313, 92.

44. Griffin, E.R. (1984) *Animal Thinking*. Harvard University Press, Cambridge, Mass.
45. Hamlyn, D.W. (1968) *Aristotle: De Anima*. Books II and III, translated with Introduction and Notes by D.W. Hamlyn. Clarendon Press, Oxford.
46. Hampshire, S. (1982) *Thought and Action*. Chatto & Windus, London.
47. Hansard, House of Commons (1984) *Animal Health and Welfare Bill*, 18th May. 60, 638. HMSO, London.
48. As above, p. 648.
49. Hardy, A. (1984) *Darwin and the Spirit of Man*. Collins, London.
50. Hardy, A. (1985) Foreword, in *Revelations: Glimpses of Reality* (ed. R.S. Lello), pp. xi–xvii. Shepheard-Walwyn, London.
51. Harrison, R. (1964) *Animal Machines*. Vincent Stuart, London.
52. Harrison, R.V. (1983) Wild; captive; dead. Wooldridge Memorial Lecture. *Veterinary Record* 113(15), 342–7.
53. Haynes, A. (1983) Murderous Millinery. *History Today*, 33, 26–30.
54. Henderson, W.M. (1981) *Man's Use of Animals*. University of Wales Press, Cardiff.
55. Hinde, R. (1985) *In litt.*
56. Hinde, R.A. and Fisher, J. (1951) Further observations on the opening of milk bottles by birds. *British Birds*. 44, 393–6.
57. Holden, C. (1981) Human-animal relationship under scrutiny. *Science*, 214, 418–420.
58. Hollands, C. (1980) *Compassion is the Bugler: the struggle for Animal Rights*. Macdonald, Edinburgh.
59. Huxley, J. (1960) Darwin Centennial Address. In *Darwin Centennial celebrations 1959* (45 papers in 3 vols). University of Chicago, Chicago.
60. Huxley, T.H. (1988) Charles Robert Darwin. Obituary: Notices of Fellows, *Proceedings of the Royal Society* 44, i–xxv.
61. Jaini, P.S. (1979). *The Jaina Path of Purification*. University of California Press, Berkeley.
62. Jakobovits, I. and Gaon, S. (1968) *Slaughter of animals for food. The Jewish method is humane*. Declaration by the Jewish Ecclesiastical Authorities of Great Britain. Board of Deputies of British Jews, London.
63. James, T.G.H. (1979) *Introduction to Ancient Egypt*. British Museum Publications, London.
64. Journal of Experimental Biology (1986) Instructions to Authors. *Journal of Experimental Biology*, 120.
65. Jung, L. (ed.) (1928) Jewish Library First Series, 1–5. Macmillan, New York.
66. Kapleau, R.P. (1983) *A Buddhist case for vegetarianism*. Rider, London.
67. Katcher, A.H. and Beck, A.M. (eds.) (1983) *New perspectives on our lives with companion animals*. University of Pennsylvania Press, Philadelphia.

68. Kettlewell, H.B.D. (1973) *The Evolution of Melanism*. Oxford University Press, Oxford.
69. Kinsey, A.C., Pomeroy, W.B. and Martin, C.E. (1948) *Sexual Behavior in the Human Male*. W.B. Saunders Co., Philadelphia.
70. Lansbury, C. (1985) *The Old Brown Dog: Women, Workers and Vivisection in Edwardian England*. University of Wisconsin Press, Wisconsin.
71. Lee, D. (1983) Pet–therapy—helping patients through troubled times. *California Vet*, 37(5), 24–5, 40.
72. Locke, John (1705) *Some thoughts concerning education*. (5E). A. & J. Churchill, London.
73. Lones, T.E. (1912) *Aristotle's Researches in Natural Science*. West, Newman & Co., London.
74. Lorenz, K. (1966) *On Aggression*. Methuen, London, p. 195.
75. Lumholtz, C. (1889) *Among Cannibals*. Scribner's, New York.
76. MacEwan, M. (1986) Hunting against the odds in Canada. *The Field*, 25 January 1986, 266, 6939, 30–1.
77. Medawar, P.B. and Medawar, J.S. (1984) *Aristotle to Zoos. A philosophical dictionary of biology*. Weidenfeld & Nicholson, London.
78. Menninger, K.A. (1951) Totemic aspects of contemporary attitudes towards animals. In *Psychoanalysis and Culture*. (eds. G. Wilbur and W. Muensterberger) pp. 42–74. International Universities Press, New York.
79. Messent, P. (1981) A review of recent developments in human-companion animal studies. *Proceedings of the Fifth Annual Kal Kan Symposium, 26–7 September 1981*, p. 27.
80. — and Horsfield, S. (1983) Pet population and the pet owner bond. *Proceedings of the Lorenz Symposium, Vienna, 27–8 October 1983*.
81. Ministry of Agriculture, Fisheries and Food (1983) *Codes of recommendations for the welfare of livestock: Cattle*. 701. HMSO, London.
82. — (1983) *Codes of recommendations for the welfare of livestock: Pigs*. 702. HMSO, London.
83. Nature (1983) What rights for animals? Anon. *Nature*, 306, 522.
84. Observer (1986) Health Harvest. *The Observer*, 5th January, 10135, p. 2.
85. Ogle, W. (1982) *Aristotle on the parts of animals*. Translated with Introduction and Notes, by W. Ogle. Kegan Paul & Co., London.
86. Pampiglione, G. (1963) *Development of cerebral function in the dog*. Butterworth, London.
87. Paton, W. (1984) *Man and Mouse. Animals in Medical Research*. Oxford University Press, Oxford.
88. Prentice, R.C. (1984) *Education and training for sporting shooting*. Unpublished report by the British Association for Shooting and Conservation, Marford Mill, Rossett, Wrexham.
89. Prior, R. (1985) Where deer are newcomers. *Game Conservancy Annual Review*, 16, 92–4.

90. Protection of Animals Act 1911 (Amendment) (1985) 12th February. HMSO, London.
91. Proust, M. (1919) *A la recherche du temps perdu*. I. *Du côté de chez Swann*. Gallimard, Paris.
92. Riegert, B. (1967) Cruelty to animals. In *New Catholic Encyclopaedia*, 4, pp. 498–9. McGraw Hill, New York.
93. Romanes, E. (ed.) (1896) *The life and letters of George John Romanes*. Longmans Green & Co., London.
94. Romanes, G.J. (1881) Letter to *The Times*, April 25th.
95. — (1883) *Mental evolution in animals*. Kegan Paul, Trench & Co., London.
96. — (1896) *A Selection from the Poems of George John Romanes*. Longmans & Co., London.
97. Rosenfield, L. (1968) *From Beast-machine to Man-machine*. Octagon Books, New York.
98. Rothschild, Miriam (1939) Hitherto unknown life-history of a trematode worm, showing its three hosts, a snail, a fish and a gull. *Royal Society Conversazione, London, 23rd June, Catalogue of Exhibits*, p. 11.
99. — (1978) Howard Hinton—the pharate adult. *Antenna*, 2, 34–6.
100. — (1979) *Nathaniel Charles Rothschild 1877–1923*. Cambridge University Press, Cambridge.
101. — (1983) *Dear Lord Rothschild. Birds, butterflies and history*. Hutchinsons, London.
102. Royal Society for the Prevention of Cruelty to Animals (1984) *161st Annual Report*. RSPCA, The Causeway, Horsham, Sussex.
103. — (1985) *The Slaughter of food animals*. RSPCA, The Causeway, Horsham, Sussex.
104. — (1985) *Animals in Schools. A compendium for teachers*. (2E) Education Department, RSPCA, The Causeway, Horsham, Sussex.
105. — (1986) RSPCA reports record animal cruelty in 1985. *News from the RSPCA, 17th February*. RSPCA, The Causeway, Horsham, Sussex.
106. Seaver, G. (1955) *Albert Schweitzer: the Man and his mind*. (5E) A. & C. Black, London.
107. Serpell, J. (1983) What have we got against pets? *New Scientist*, 13 October, 80–4.
108. Singer, P. (1975) *Animal Liberation*. Random House, New York.
109. Skinner, B.F. (1974) *About Behaviorism*. Random House, New York.
110. Smith, R. and Willey, K. (1969) *New Guinea*. Lansdowne, Melbourne.
111. Spencer, Herbert (1868) *Social statics; or, The conditions essential to human happiness specified, and the first of them developed*, p. 451. Williams & Norgate, London.
112. Swiss Society for the Protection of Animals (1977) *Das Sogennante Schächtverbot*. 6. Swiss Society for the Protection of Animals, Basel.

113. Tabor, R. (1983) *The Wildlife of the domestic cat*. Arrow Books, London.
114. Terrace, H.S. (1985) Animal cognition: thinking without language. *Philosophical Transactions of the Royal Society*, **308**, 113–28.
115. Thomas, K. (1983) *Man and the Natural World*. Allen Lane, London.
116. Waddington, C.H. (1960) *The Ethical Animal*. Allen & Unwin, London.
117. Wallace, A.R. (1864). The origin of the human races and the antiquity of man deduced from the theory of 'Natural Selection'. *Anthropological Review*, **2**, (clviii–clxx, discussion clxx–clxxxvii).
118. Wildlife and Countryside Act (1981) Public and General Acts and Measures of 1981, Part II. Chapter 69, 2145–272. HMSO, London.
119. Wilson, C.A. (1984) *Food and Drink in Britain from the Stone Age to Recent Times*. Penguin Books, Harmondsworth.
120. Wynne-Tyson, J. (ed.) (1985) *The Extended Circle. A Dictionary of Humane Thought*. Centaur Press, Fontwell.

GENERAL READING

Armstrong, E.A. (1973) *Saint Francis: Nature Mystic*. University of California Press, Berkeley.

ATLA, Alternatives to laboratory animals. Published by the Fund for the Replacement of Animals in Medical Experiments, Nottingham.

Beny, R. and Matheson, S. (1984) *Rajasthan*. Muller Ltd., London.

Boas, G. (1973) Theriophily. In *Dictionary of the History of Ideas*, IV. (ed. P.P. Weiner) pp. 384–9. Scribner's, New York.

Brodie, J.D. (1981) Health benefits of owning pet animals. *Veterinary Record*, 109, 10, 197–9.

Burkhardt, F. and Smith, S. (1985) *A Calendar of the Correspondence of Charles Darwin 1821–1882*. Garland Press, New York.

Carnell, P. (1983) *Alternatives to Factory Farming. An economic appraisal*. Earth Resources Research Ltd., London.

Carpenter, E. (1980) *Animals and Ethics*. A report of the working party chaired by the Very Rev. Dr. Edward Carpenter. Watkins, London.

Cohen, N.J. (1976) *Tsa'ar Ba'ale Hayim. The Prevention of Cruelty to animals*. Feldheim, Jerusalem.

Crook, J.H. (1983) On attributing consciousness to animals. *Nature*, 303, 11–14.

Drengson, A.R. (1980) Social and psychological implications of human attitudes towards animals. *Journal of Transpersonal Psychology* 12, 1, 63–74.

Ewbank, R. (1985) The behavioural needs of farm and laboratory animals. In *Animal Experimentation: Improvements and Alternatives, Replacement, Refinement and Reduction*, pp. 31–7. Proceedings of a Symposium organized by the Liverpool Ethical Group. ATAL Supplement.

Fogle, B. (ed.) (1981) *Interrelations between people and pets*. C.C. Thomas, Springfield, Illinois.

Fox, M.W. and Mickley, L.D. (eds.) (1984) *Advances in Animal Welfare Science 1984/5*. The Humane Society of the United States, Washington D.C.

Frame News. Newsletter of the Fund for the Replacement of Animals in Medical Experiments. Frame, Nottingham.

Griffin, D.R. (1981) *The Question of Animal Awareness*. (Revised ed.) P. Rockefeller, California.

Hafez, E.S.E. (ed.) (1962) *The behaviour of domestic animals*. Bailliére Tindall & Cox, London.

Hampson, Judith (1982) Laboratory animals—our responsibility. *RSPCA Today*, 41, 36–7.

Hardy, A. (1967) Biology and Extra Sensory Perception. In *Science and ESP* (ed. J.R. Smythies), pp. 143–64. Routledge & Kegan Paul, London.

Klingender, F. (1971) *Animals in Art and Thought*. Routledge & Kegan Paul, London.

Lapage, G. (1960) *Achievement*. Heffer & Sons, Cambridge.

Levi, L. (1983) *Torah and Science. Their interplay in the world scheme*. Feldheim Publishers, Jerusalem.

Midgley, M. (1983) *Animals and why they matter*. Penguin Books, Harmondsworth.

North, R. (1983) *The Animals Report*. Penguin Books, Harmondsworth.

Patmore, A. (1984) *Your Obedient Servant. The story of Man's Best Friend*. Hutchinson, London.

Regan, T. (1983) *The case for Animal Rights*. University of California Press, Berkeley.

Renou, L. (1953) *Religions of Ancient India*. Athlone Press, London.

Romanes, G.J. (1882) *Animal Intelligence*. Kegan Paul Trench, & Co., London.

—— (1888) *Mental Evolution in Man*. Kegan Paul, Trench & Co., London.

—— (1892-7) *Darwin, and after Darwin*. I-III. Longmans Green, London.

Royal Society for the Prevention of Cruelty to Animals. *Annual Reports*. 1982-1986. RSPCA, The Causeway, Horsham, Sussex.

—— (1984) *Policies on animal welfare* (Revised edn.). RSPCA, The Causeway, Horsham, Sussex.

Scottish Society for the Prevention of Vivisection (1986) *Annual Pictorial Review 1986*. Seventy-fourth Annual Report for year ending 31st December 1985. Scottish Society for the Prevention of Vivisection, Edinburgh.

Serpell, J. (1986) *In the company of animals*. Basil Blackwell, Oxford.

Smythies, J.R. (ed.) (1967) *Science and ESP*. Routledge & Kegan Paul, London.

Terrace, H.S. (1979) *Nim*. Alfred A. Knopf, New York.

—— (1984) Animal cognition. In *Animal Cognition* (ed. H.L. Roitblat, T.G. Bever and H.S. Terrace) pp. 7-28. Lawrence Erlbaum Associates, Hillsdale, New Jersey.

—— (1984) Animal learning, ethology and biological constraints. In *The Biology of Learning* (ed. P. Marler and H.S. Terrace) pp. 15-45. Springer-Verlag, New York.

Universities Federation for Animal Welfare (1984-5) *Reports and Accounts*. Universities Federation for Animal Welfare, South Mimms, Potters Bar.

Walker, S. (1983) *Animal Thought*. Routledge & Kegan Paul, London.

Weiskrantz, L. (ed.) (1985) Animal Intelligence. Proceedings of a Royal Society Discussion meeting, 6-7 June, 1984. *Philosophical Transactions of the Royal Society of London*, 308, 1-216.

Wood-Gush, D.G.M., Dawkins, M. and Ewbank, R. (1981) (eds.) Self-awareness in domesticated animals. *Proceedings of the Workshop held at Keble College, Oxford, 7-8 July, 1980*. Universities Federation for Animal Welfare, South Mimms, Potters Bar.

Zahn-Waxler, C., Hollenbeck, S. and Radke-Garrow, M. (1984) The origins of empathy and altruism. In *Advances in Animal Welfare*

Science 1984/5 (M.W. Fox and L.D. Mickley, eds.), pp. 21-59. The Humane Society of the United States, Washington, D.C.

Zoophilist (1881) *Special Supplement* 1, 2 May, pp. 17-24, London.

INDEX